never *said*

never *said*

BY

CAROL LYNCH WILLIAMS

BLINK

For LuAnn

annie

If
     they
          knew.

annie

At the foot of my bed
is the nightmare.
A silhouette
watching   waiting
for me.

sarah

Here's how it ended.

"Sarah, we're too serious."

It was late. After dusk. This past October, when the skies teemed with snow clouds and we wondered if this would be a bad winter.

I couldn't see the stars. Words caught in my throat. Stuck there. Garret's words had pinned them.

"What do you mean?"

He stood next to me but I almost couldn't see him. Just his outline. A silhouette.

He held my hand, his fingers loose. "We have to make room for other people," he said, and for a moment I wondered if I was dreaming. The wind blew, and I felt chilled through, like the air touched my bones. The parts of me that had slipped away when I became comfortable with Garret dropped onto my shoulders one by one. I wanted to run, get away. Not listen.

"What are you saying?" I asked. "I don't understand."

Garret straightened. I looked up at him. His features weren't clear in the darkness, but I'd memorized the green eyes, the blond color of his hair, that smile.

He didn't smile now, though. "We need a break. We need to

see if we're right for each other." The words flowed from him like they were someone else's.

It was too much pressure, he said.

(Did he mean I was too much pressure? That we together were? That we didn't work, though I was sure, was positive, we did? How could his words shake me up so?)

His mother was always on his back, he said.

He had to date other people, he said.

And that was that.

After more than eighteen months of being together, of being a couple. After I gave my heart to him. Nearly everything I had. After all that, he decided to look elsewhere.

monday

sarah

I saw it, Annie." Mom's talking. Intent.

They've waited on dinner for me, and I slip into my chair, late.

Annie doesn't answer our mother. She fills her plate. Careful. Making sure nothing touches on the china. Neat compartments.

"Annie?"

"Mom?"

Dad looks at them from the end of the table. Every night, Mom sets out a meal like this. She used to run her own catering business and, as she says, "A pretty table is in my blood."

I dish the roast beef and onions and potatoes out. The aroma of the food swirls around in the air. "What's going on?" I ask.

Dad shrugs. "Girl things, Sarah," he says.

I raise my eyebrows at him. "Uh, Dad?"

Then he winks. *Oh*. Those girl things. I go silent.

Mom folds her napkin. "Annie was invited to sit as a judge on a Junior League beauty contest."

Annie and Mom. For two people so similar, their expressions are opposite. One face blank. The other animated.

"She opened my mail," Annie says to me.

"Oh."

"I suggested," Mom says, "she drop a few pounds in preparation." Mom stirs butter into the potatoes. "I think she should do it. Be an example to these young girls."

I glance at Annie, who stares toward the fireplace. There's a snap of burning logs, and sparks slip up the chimney.

Dad says, "Are you kidding? What an honor. You were the best, now weren't you, Annie?"

My sister.

The talented one. With all the promise in the world. Now she's the silent one.

My sister is heavy. She looks different than Before. That's what fat does to you. Her hair isn't blonde like it was. She's traded pageant dresses for sweats, but she's still beautiful. She has the same perfect, creamy skin. Her eyes sparkle. Her teeth are perfect. When she smiles, you know she means it.

But Annie's not smiling now.

"Did you hear me?" Mom says. "It's not for two more months, not till April fifteenth."

"Tax day," Dad says, and his phone, sitting on the table next to his wine glass, buzzes.

"You could drop a few pounds by then." Mom takes a breath. "Maybe participate again."

Annie doesn't seem to notice our mother. But I see her flinch and it's like I flinch too.

Twins. Twins are supposed to feel the same. Look the same. Are supposed to be the same. Right?

If she won't speak, I can. I get not wanting to do something even if you're the best. Mom has to know things have changed. For Annie. For all of us.

I draw in a breath. "Mom?" I say when Annie stays quiet. I jab at a raw spinach leaf. I'm annoyed. At Annie for staying quiet. At Mom for saying these stupid things. At Dad for getting on his phone. He's talking to someone. There's an almost-smile on his lips. "Mom, Annie gave that up. Remember?"

Mom's surprised. Like Annie hasn't said she's not interested in the pageant world a hundred times over the last few months. "What do you mean, Sarah? That Annie won't judge? That she'll never be a part of that again?"

Dad excuses himself and strides over to the fire. "Jim, good to hear from you!"

I can do this. "Well," I say, but Mom stares away from me, that napkin of hers clenched in her fist. I can't drag in enough air to satisfy this fight. So I think the words.

You are so impossible lately, Mom. And Dad is too absent. And Annie, you ... you're doing nothing but eating.

It's true. Right now she's eating in slow, perfect, exact movements.

The whole family is strained. Stretched at the edges. The stitching hanging loose. It's been this way for ages now. Since the Weight.

Dad doesn't finish his plate. Doesn't look over at us, he's that engaged with Jim.

When I say, "Come on, Mom," my voice comes out whispery. Taut. "You don't need to suggest diets. Annie's a big girl."

Wait. I didn't mean that. Big is the wrong thing to say. I feel my face color.

Dad gives everyone a thumbs-up. He comes back to the table. "Gotta work," he says. As he turns toward the other end of the house, where his home office is, I hear, "Don't forget we're having that party here Saturday night."

Oh. That.

Great.

annie

A tradition we
have kept
my whole life
whether all of us have
wanted to or
not — is
these (now) insane mealtimes
together.

Consistency
Soldiers our family. Makes
Us do what we should
What we're told

Family time
Family dinner
Family parties

Meals are a joke.
No one listens to anyone.
We all talk — except Sarah — and not one of us
hears.

Sometimes
      when I look around at us
sitting together,
      see who we've become,
I'm surprised that
notthatlongago
we
were related: a family. Happy.
         Now
      we
are separates.
Mismatched.

More family moments
      my father insists on,
      demands
are the parties.

I used to love them.

Mom developed the menu,
Sarah practiced violin all over the house (when there was
no one near)
I went with Dad to order flowers
and send out invitations
      (nothing Internet —
      just old-fashioned mail).

Yes, I used to love them.

Sarah, though,
          has hated it all
since the beginning.
          Hates the show we put on
hates serving
appetizers,
speaking to strangers
(she has a hard enough time
speaking out
communicating
talking
to us).

Now —
I agree with my sister.
          Fat and thin.
          Night and day.
          Angry and silent.
Let's drop the show we put on for everyone.

None of us are who we say we are.

sarah

At the table, I wonder: Would I be different if I could talk to strangers without wanting to throw up, could stand at a microphone and not feel like I was having a heart attack, could remember public events (like school and office parties and church) without an anxiety attack?

Would I be different if I hadn't broken up with Garret King?

Yes, it was two months ago. Yes, young love doesn't matter, isn't real. But I still feel raw, still feel pain, still feel awful.

Would I be different if my parents thought more of me (the ugly duckling) and less of Annie (who was so lovely that adult men gasped)?

"I think …" I have to clear my throat.

Would this be different?

What if they looked at us like equals?

"I think …" I say. But there are no more words. I glance up from my plate in time to see Dad sort of smile at my sister as he leaves. It's fake, that smile. One I have seen aimed at me, at Mom, at people he tolerates. I swallow, but nothing wants to go down.

Annie stares at me. She raises an eyebrow, and I'm not sure of the code. What's she saying? Before I can figure it out, Mom says, "I told them yes, Annie. That you'd do it."

My sister? No response. She just eats.

sarah

Dad's left his plate and coffee cup on the table. Mom seems so … alone.

I'm startled by her expression.

"Remember," she says, like she doesn't notice her husband leaving when I can see she does, "when you would pageant? Do you remember that, Annie? You would be such an inspiration for the youngsters."

Annie nods. "That was only last year, Mom," she says. "Of course I remember." The heat kicks on. I breathe in deep and smell the homemade rolls. "No one forgets the pageants. Do we, Sarah?"

I shake my head, hiding behind hair that corkscrews over my shoulder. Does my sister know how I felt about all that Annie Time? All the Winning Time? The Stand-on-the-Stage-and-Accept-the-Trophy time? I had hoped I'd hidden that. "I remember," I say. "You never lost."

My sister looks surprised. Why? Because I know her history? Or because I speak of it?

"She's right," Mom says. "You never lost, Annie." Mom leans forward, hands clasped. "Think of those little girls, all dressed up."

"Mom," Annie says.

The chandelier is too bright.

"Glad I don't have to do that," I say.

"Speak up, please, Sarah," Mom says. "Not to yourself. To everyone."

I don't have the energy to get into it now. There's too much tension. I tighten my lips like they're sewn together.

Annie won't participate in the judging. I know it. Mom should too.

"No, thanks," I say, answering Mom, but she's focused on Annie.

Maybe Mom does know the answer.

Here's a truth: Before.

Before, I was terrified our Mom might force me to pageant. Believe me, there are lots of good things about being a normal-looking girl. Nothing on me is exquisite. No almond-shaped eyes. No heart-shaped face. No natural highlights.

Green eyes. Flat chest. Short.

Plain.

My looks kept me in the audience. Away from the stage.

Thank goodness. Oh, thank goodness.

Still, I close my eyes, remembering. Sorry. I was jealous of all the attention my sister got. It takes effort to admit this to myself. It's embarrassing. But I was jealous of being so lost. So left behind.

Now I glance up at Mom and Annie.

"I don't understand," Mom's saying.

Annie's done with her first helping, her plate almost spotless. That nursery rhyme pops in my head, the one about Jack Spratt. "...and so betwixt the two of them, they licked the platter clean." She reaches for more Jell-O with carrots. Stares at Mom as she spoons some onto her plate.

How can she stand it? This weight talk? I would leave, eat alone, never sit with anyone. Not even my family.

"Have you ever thought your constant jabber may be why I keep eating?" Annie says.

Everything in the room slows. The clock, our breathing, the beating of our hearts. It all seems to stop and wait for Mom to answer. These rhythms beat out of time.

I can see Annie and me in the French doors, broken into pieces by the panes of glass.

"How *dare* you? I am not the reason for your bad decision making." Mom huffs then glares at me, me, like I'm the problem. "I don't know when you became so unkind." Like I just hurt her feelings. Or gained the weight.

annie

If you eat
      long enough
           hard enough
                more than enough
you can do what needs to be done.

At first I didn't
realize.
I ate
      because creamy chocolate
      gooey caramel
      salted, buttery popcorn
made me feel
better.

A few pounds   *a few pounds more*
and
I am in control.

sarah

That's when it started. The changing. All of us. Changing.

With Annie's weight gain came Dad staying away and Mom talking too much.

Before was different.

Before, we always did Annie Family Stuff.

Before, there was me, keeping where I'm most comfortable … in the background. With a book. At home. Quiet. Observing.

However, home is no longer comfortable.

That's the connection, I realize, sitting here. Watching our mother stand, leave her dishes behind, follow Dad to wherever. Her face red, her eyes tearing up.

We've been stuck in Annie's fat since the first pound.

sarah

This must be hard, I think, having two broken daughters.

sarah

I climb the stairs to my room.
Outside, the storm rages and an unknown fear shuttles across my chest.

I squeeze my eyes shut. Open them.

The carpet catches any sounds my shoes might have made.

I speak to myself. There's no one to hear. I can say what I want. Whisper if I want, raise my voice if I want. "I'm not the same as my sister."

Annie loved winning. Loved the crowds. Playing the piano in front of the world. She got what she wanted then.

Still does.

Even in this crazy world she's created, Annie gets what she wants. She sneaks downstairs at night to eat. Gets up before everyone to make breakfast. Packs a lunch big enough for two or three. We were the same size. Same weight. That was Before. Now we're twins who are different.

"It's not fair." As the words come out I know I sound like a baby. But …

She wanted pageants. She got that.

Now she wants to eat, so she does.

And me? I wanted Garret. And he's gone. Tears burn my eyes. My head hurts.

How is that right?

sarah

The snowstorm batters the house and trees bow in the wind. As I get ready for bed, I hear Mom. She's after Annie. Again. Or still. I'm not sure which.

I peek out my bedroom and see Mom down the hall, in Annie's doorway. The walls are lined with photos. Pageant pictures, most of them. Some of us as a family. A few of me and Annie when we were little. On the beach. At the park. Black and white. Color. It's a tunnel of photographs.

"Do you know," Mom says, "what your father and I have done for you? How we've sacrificed?"

A part of me wants to shout, to holler, "Let it go. Leave her alone already." But I'll never yell. The thought of confrontation makes my skin cool. My lips tingle.

Mom glances at me, like she's heard my thoughts. "And Sarah too." She waves her hand in my direction.

I duck into my room but stand where I can hear everything. Why does Mom keep going on? She hasn't pestered Annie this way in a while. Is it the chance to get back into the business of pageants? Even if only as a judge? Has Annie gained a pound or two more and can Mom see that?

"We've all given up our lives for you. Helped you win scholarships and trophies and …" Mom's frustration bleeds down the hall. I peer out at her. See the annoyance in her face. Hear it in her voice. It's dripping off her. Puddling on the floor.

Why hasn't Annie run off like Dad always manages to do? She's resilient, my sister. She has endurance.

"The doctors keep saying there's no reason you should be gaining all this weight."

I can't see my sister, but I hear her when she finally answers. Her voice is full of sarcasm. "As if everything can be found by a doctor looking into your ears."

The wind picks up, whistling like it agrees with Annie.

I'm punctured by the sound of Annie's words. They're naked.

"Guess what, Mom?" Annie says. "I'm fat. What's a forty-five pound weight gain in a year or so?"

That much? She's gained that much?

"You were so pretty," Mom says. The words echo against the walls. Hit our home stronger than the storm. Colder. The comment isn't directed at me, but it stings. I gasp for my sister. Feel the cut in my own heart. I peek back down the hall, wanting to walk to Annie. Stand beside. Hold her hand, if she'll let me.

There's a long pause. The whole house tries to catch its breath.

"Are you saying," Annie says, "because I'm fat, I'm not pretty anymore?"

Miles separate us, but I can see her hurt.

There's a fist in my throat.

Mom says nothing. Instead she twists her wedding ring around her slim finger then walks away. As she passes she says, "You helped start this."

"Me?" Wait.

But Mom holds her hand up in my face and disappears into her room.

Annie's voice is blizzard loud. "Are you saying that fat makes a person ugly?"

No answer from Mom, except the shutting of her door.

The lock clicks.

I stand quiet. Still. The carpet is so soft. Annie looks at me.

For a second I remember sharing a bed when we were young — laughing, telling secrets, sleeping snuggled together, maybe like in the womb.

She says, "This is the way I want to be." Proud.

Then she closes the door and I hear that lock click too.

annie

*What makes a girl
beautiful?*

*What makes
me
beautiful?*

sarah

We are torn up. Torn apart. No longer who we were. We are stuck in Annie's fat. Stuck in Mom's anger. Stuck in Dad's job.

Me. Alone. Again.

There's not a sound anywhere until, from downstairs, I hear the grandfather clock calling out the time. Like I'm released from a spell, I retreat into my room and flick the light out, lie down on my bed, and just wait.

annie

In the bathroom
I strip off my clothes and stare at   me.

I am disgusting
sickening
Fat

fat like Mom says
as ugly as I know I look when Dad sees   me.

If the lights were on I
could see tears drip from my face

the way I used to watch myself cry
when I was little
(when I thought I could be a movie star   me).

Instead, I pinch bruises
along my thighs
where my family
won't see
them

sarah

I stare at the ceiling, where leftover stars glow. Annie and I put some in my room, some in hers, years ago when we first moved here.

Now, when I close my eyes, I see the stars still. Pale. Almost not there.

I feel so not here. Like these failing stars. I am invisible and have been for years. Since Annie blossomed and I slipped out of sight.

Thin, she's a star herself. Fat, she still draws attention.

I roll on my side. My sister's crushed by our mom and I lie here thinking about me.

Selfish. This is so selfish.

But I can't help it.

annie

Left-handed anger
pushes down
spilling over
and free
Unacceptable thoughts.
Hurt
Kill
Now I lay me down to sleep
I pray I pray I pray
for
A place for people like me
The outcasts
The lepers
The untouchables.
All of us
The fat, too skinny
the gays, left-out straight
the awkward, the lonely, graceful.
The ones only Christ sees.

tuesday

sarah

Tuesday morning dawns snowy cold. I lie in bed. Stretch. From where I am I can see the indigo sky.

"Beautiful," I whisper to the stars that don't glow anymore. Maybe it's time to remove those things.

I stand. Stretch again. Think school, and my stomach falls near my heels. No snow days here unless ice covers everything (we're winter stock, laughing when other parts of the country get a foot or two of snow and whine).

How I'd love to stay home and play violin. Or linger in bed and read or make hot chocolate from Hershey candy bars and thick vanilla cream.

School means I can't stay home and wonder at nothing. I've got to go.

Morning pushes at the window with its fingertips, like it wants in to warm up. The street lights are pumpkin bulbs. My room is the color of a black-and-white photo.

I shiver, and then … then … I stand at the window and watch.

This is the time Garret leaves for school.

His house is settled on the corner opposite ours. I see his window from mine, and for a moment it's like I'm in some scene from an old romantic novel where the girl gets the boy.

I wrap my arms around myself. In almost all the books I read, the girl does get the boy. Except that doesn't happen here. It won't.

He has the shades drawn, but I can see movement behind them, and I remember the afternoon (it feels so long ago!) he snuck me into his bedroom when his mother turned her back, and we watched movies on his flat screen.

"Garret. It's awfully quiet up there." His mom. Her feet on the stairs, coming closer.

Me tiptoeing to the bathroom, stepping into the tub, my heart pounding. Garret opening his door to her saying, "I'm sixteen, Mom. I can watch *Raiders of the Lost Ark* without making any noise."

Then his door shut. I didn't move. Instead I stayed there, wanting to laugh, excitement coursing through every part of me.

That was my first kiss. Standing in his tub. So weird that I would sneak over to a guy's house and get my first kiss in his bathroom. It was all awkward and his lips were warm and he had to push the shower curtain out of the way and I felt silly and thrilled and not even afraid because this moment was worth it.

Now his light goes out and I jump, then duck. Like he can see me.

Does he even look this way? Does he ever think of me in the tub that day after his mother left, the two of us laughing without sound, staring at each other wide-eyed when he helped me out, holding hands?

I felt sure we'd get caught.

And I didn't care.

Now, I can't quite breathe, remembering.

I touch the glass, feel tears rise again

again

again.

I love him. I still love him.

sarah

I climb back into bed.

Force myself to stop thinking of anything. Of everything.

Nothing outside my home should matter. Not right now.

I think of last night. My mother. My sister. Their fight in the hall with words just above whispers.

Can I see both sides? The question of both, yes.

Like no answers for Annie's weight gain? Sometimes Mom is just dumb. It's kind of funny. Not funny ha-ha, either, that our mother is willing to be blind. All the weird crap, and Mom thinks the idea of a diet will change things.

Annie eats. Simple as that.

I swallow. What more drives my sister?

I asked her why she had stopped exercising, in the beginning when Mom was freaking out over ten pounds, and Annie shrugged. "I'm cool," she said. Like she could care less. Then she closed her mouth to me.

There are answers for my issues, however. Mom made sure to find those.

When I wouldn't go places unless forced, refused to give talks in class, when I didn't make friends but stayed safe with books. When I threw up from fear, couldn't leave my room, and wouldn't come down for dinner sometimes, Mom took me to the doctor.

He did check my ears. My eyes. Listened to my heart. And listened to Mom.

I couldn't answer his questions. It seemed a hand clasped my throat the whole time we were in the office.

"A case of social anxiety," Dr. McArthur had said. He looked at me over the top of his glasses. Patted my knee. Smiled a real smile.

"So she needs to do more?" Mom said. "Put herself out there? Work through it? I used to be shy."

Dr. McArthur rested against a counter that held a jar of extra-long cotton swabs. He kept watching me. All over the walls were *Where the Wild Things Are* pictures. Taken straight from the book and blown up big. If I could have snuck to that place where Max was, I would have.

"I think she'll find more success if she practices deep breathing. Find things to help her relax. What do you say to meditation, Sarah?"

I'd pulled one of my fingernails into the quick and now it bled. I ducked my head.

"It's okay, Sarah. We'll help you," Dr. McArthur said, and he'd handed Mom pamphlets to look over and gave her a list of other doctors for me to see.

I went to a therapist for a while. Did deep breathing. Got a prescription for Xanax for when things get really bad.

But the truth is that it's still hard. Still. Now.

Every day, I have to make myself do things that other people think are normal. Like going to school. Even years later, after so many doctors. I'm still afraid people are watching me. I'm afraid I'll do something to embarrass myself. I'm scared of being alone — almost as much as I am of being with others.

I don't want to be noticed for anything.

So I stay in my head.

The only time I felt good, happy, and whole was with Garret.

annie

I had every guy I ever wanted
no matter who he was with,
no matter if I knew his girlfriend,
no matter if I really wanted him
or not.

And
I watch my sister
(she seems so little
so not there
too thin)
come down the stairs
in the mornings.

She's been watching him.
I want to tell her not to.
To look away.
Let him go.
But Sarah can't seem to.

sarah

Driving in with me?" Annie asks. She doesn't look up from the over-medium eggs, bacon, and hash browns. With care, she piles a mixed bite on buttered toast and eats like nothing in the world tastes better.

How does she know I'm here without looking? Does she sense me near? Does she feel the air in the room change? Hear my heartbeat?

Doctors say some twins can do that—sense the other. I've even heard of twins who do the same things even if they're in different states, thousands of miles away.

"If you're on time," I say. I hate to drive. I only do it if I must.

Annie has a habit of being late. This used to be her only flaw—that she was late everywhere. Now, sometimes, she doesn't even show up.

"You're still in jammies."

"So are you." Annie chews. Swallows. Winks at me in this over-exaggerated way. Like winking is normal.

I can't help it. I smile. "Where's the Cap'n Crunch?"

Annie turns till she's almost looking at me. "Mom hid it in the lazy Susan. She's watching out for me."

"Of course."

A gust of wind hits the house with a slap. And then, like the wind brought it, Annie says, "Stop torturing yourself, Sarah." Her voice is raised, like she's trying to talk over the cries of winter.

I step toward my sister. Change my mind, because what would I do if I sat next to her? Instead I grab the cereal box and gather a bowl and milk and a spoon. Take a deep breath, think. Answer her.

Somehow I know what she means, but I pretend I have no idea what Annie's talking about. "What?"

My next breath catches somewhere in my chest.

"It's eating you alive."

I can't nod. Don't swallow. Refuse to think.

"Let him go. Don't give him that power."

We stare at each other a good fifteen seconds. The only light in this area is over the bar where Annie sits. I smell the eggs and browned butter and think, *Why does she have to know how I feel? We're twins separated by a thousand miles and she knows how I feel.*

"Forget him, Sarah." She's whispering now.

I'm on autopilot. No longer want to eat. I put everything away. Make myself a glass of milk chocolate Carnation Instant Breakfast.

I can't look at Annie.

How? How can I not think of Garret? How do I forget him?

"I don't want to forget," I say. The words fall out of my mouth like chips of glass.

"I get it." She nods. "I do."

We're quiet again and I change my mind about where to sit. Move to the chair right next to hers.

"I get it."

There is no way she understands how I feel. I know for a fact. She's had more boyfriends, dates, flings, meaningful library romances than all her girlfriends combined. Resentment wants to put up a wall between us.

"I have something else I need to talk to you about," she says.

"No more." I hold up my hand. I should have chosen strawberry. Maybe that wouldn't taste like liquid cardboard.

"Not about you." Annie licks her fingers. She's a study in eating, the way the light shines on her. "It's been nagging at me."

I swallow the rest of the drink. Will I throw up? I have to calm myself to keep from gagging, breathe through my nose to stay in control.

"I was awake all night," Annie says. "Thinking. Worrying about something Mom said."

"Okay." My voice is thin. My breath releases.

Annie's hands tremble, "Not now. Later? Maybe at lunch?"

We haven't eaten together at school since sixth grade. This must be something momentous, if Annie is willing to hang out with me at school. Like there's a broken window somewhere in the house, I feel a blast of cold.

"Sure," I say, and work to steady my heart.

sarah

My sister knows too much about my feelings. I hate that. But I love it too.

Mom has never once asked me why Garret doesn't visit anymore. She hasn't stopped outside my door at night, given me any looks of concern. Maybe she doesn't know I cried (still cry) because he broke up with me. Does she even know it happened? Does she care?

Sheesh. Saying it makes me sound like an idiot. An idiot girl who loves someone who chose not to love her back.

I hurry upstairs to get dressed.

I thought I would marry him. And yes, I know that no one finds their Prince Charming first thing. We're not supposed to.

But Garret and I talked about it. About marriage.

I thought it would happen after high school. Sometime during college when I went off to major in Deaf Studies and he did law. I thought we would spend the rest of our lives together. Have babies. Lots of babies.

They would have been so pretty.

annie

My sister doesn't know enough.

annie

I'm alone
in
this house,
in my life.

For years I wanted
to share the spotlight.
Not be the only star
of the family.
To shine the attention
at my sister,
who has been lost from sight
all this time.

Getting what you wish for
hope for
want
always comes with a price, doesn't it?

sarah

As I go through my closet looking for something to wear (something easy, something like my mood) I think how I used to be angry with Annie. Sometimes I'm still bothered that she has all the attention. Negative or positive, attention is attention.

I pause, struck with an odd memory.

Once, we went shopping. Me and Annie and Mom and Dad. All of us. Not just your casual let's-run-to-the-mall thing. Annie needed a gown, and that meant some upscale shops in Riverwoods downtown.

Annie ended up trying on half the dresses in one store while I was left to read in a chair in the dressing room, and somehow — somehow — they forgot me.

Forgot to take me home.

Two kids, and Mom and Dad left me tucked between billows of color reading *The Window*.

I stood in front of that shop for thirty minutes, alone, waiting. Then Dad came screeching around the corner, driving the Escalade up on the sidewalk, and Mom scooped me up in her arms. I felt her breath on my face. Her tears on my cheeks. Heard her mumbled words of sorry.

Annie grinned in my face and said, "I told them to go back for you."

Such an odd feeling that day. Worried they might not find me. Worried they would.

I could have walked home, if I'd wanted.

But for a few minutes I hadn't felt the pressure of dress shopping. Or looking at this style and that one.

Sure, Mom and Dad forgot me. But I hadn't minded that much.

Now I wade through clothes, my hands running over silk sweaters and a cashmere jacket. Annie's closet, on the other hand, is jammed, though she wears only the outfits she recently purchased from a thrift shop. (She still has all her dresses from pageanting. Boxes piled at the top of her closet, gowns the colors of the rainbow inside them.)

Smiling a little at the memory, I push through my clothing. How sick am I if my family bothers me that much and I don't mind being left behind?

What to wear? What to wear?

I can't decide.

What outfit would Mom suggest for me?

I pause. Annie's so much like our mom — even now. Beautiful. Smart. The two love the same movies. Both were cheerleaders. Both did the pageant thing. Both were popular.

Digging through the back of my closet, I find a shirt of Dad's. I haven't seen it in forever. It's another Before memory, from when the family felt more comfortable. I pull the old flannel out and press it to my face. Tears sting my eyes.

"You'll be okay, Sarah," I whisper to myself. Whisper into the shirt. "Get dressed."

I glance into the mirror. It's silly. Me in my underwear holding Dad's clothing. But I love how this shirt is too big for me. How soft it feels. How the greens and blues look against my skin. How it absorbs tears.

I put the shirt on, then my jeans. Pull on socks. Boots.

Down the hall, Annie's getting ready. I hear her humming inside our shared bathroom.

I sit on the edge of my bed. Dab at my eyes. I'm tired from thinking. Without looking in the mirror, I fix my hair. It's crazy curly and I don't even try to comb through it, instead just pull the whole mess up into a ponytail.

Should I take the time to put on makeup?

I glance at myself side-eyed. "I want Mom and Dad to like me," I say to the reflection. As much as they love my vibrant sister. The spoken thought makes my throat tighten. Tears again spring to my eyes. I sigh. Better take meds to school with me.

"They love you," I say, getting a pill from the bottle and popping it without water. And they do. I know that.

sarah

On our way to school, snow falling like feathers, Annie says, "There's Mr. Freeman. He's outside every morning." She's whispering, like he might hear us if she used her whole voice. She pulls her jacket tighter at her throat. "Did you know that?"

I look up from *Everything Is Fine*. "Not really," I say. "I've never really noticed."

"That's 'cause you always have your head in a book."

True.

Annie slows and we both look at our down-the-street neighbor. "It's like he's watching us."

"Watching us? No. He's shoveling his driveway." I stare at Mr. Freeman. He's bent over his work. Snowflakes cling to his head and shoulders. "Gosh, I hope he doesn't freeze out there."

"It's gotta be below zero," Annie says. "Why would he be doing this now? He's a freak."

I glance at my sister. Her face is like stone, like she's frozen. With gloved hands I cover my mouth and nose then blow out to warm my face a little.

This is a bitter winter. Amazing ski conditions at all the slopes, snowdrifts piled higher than the mailboxes here in the valley, and me feeling closed in. I like it. There's an almost safe feeling. Like no one can get you. Like no one can see you.

We drive on.

In slow motion, the winter sky comes to life as sticklike fingers of the sun begin to push at the dark. We pass our neighbor, who seems to move only teaspoons full of snow at a time.

"He's not that bad," I say to Annie. "He's just a lonely old man." I remember when Mr. Freeman's wife died. Annie played the piano at the funeral. He cried the whole service.

"Whatever," she says, then peels off, sliding this way and that until she gets control of the car.

I laugh with surprise.

Annie bares her teeth.

Half a mile from school, my heart starts pounding. Pounding the way that makes you sick to your stomach. Pounding the way it's done all my life.

The radio blasts out classical music. (Yes, classical. Annie and I both love it. Play it. I even read music scores when I'm bored.) I close my eyes. Try to let the music calm me. Why? Why can't I get used to this? Going to school, going to work, being in public. Normal people do it. Why can't I?

Annie's singing along with Mozart. No words. But still she sings. Off-key as ever. I just want to stay in the car with her forever.

I know, though, once you're in public, if you're quiet, people won't see you. If you keep your hand down in class, people won't make fun of your answers. If you walk at the edge of the hallway, people (as a rule) won't run into you.

There are ways to stay out of the way. Never answer a question. Don't volunteer anything. Sit near the back of the classroom. When called upon, keep answers short. Make yourself smaller in your desk. Don't lean forward in anticipation. Move around if there are no assigned seats.

Think invisible. Become invisible.

I'll be okay. I will. I know I will.

And I'll try and do what Annie has said. Not even think of Garret, though just knowing I'll see him today keeps me alive and kills me at the same time.

sarah

Remember to give it a break," Annie says, reading my mind again. She turns off the car. Looks at me. Smiles right in my face. She licks her finger and runs it over my left eyebrow, then right.

My throat closes up at her touch. "I don't like spit on my face," I say. Sort of. The words aren't really there. But I don't move away from my sister.

She cups my face in her hands.

"Okay," I say.

Something inside me warms at her touch. My sister and me the same, right at this moment.

I say it again. "Okay." Then I close my eyes.

I sit in the car, not moving, after she leaves. The interior grows cold now that the engine and heat are off. I'll let go if I have to, but I'm not ready yet to stop thinking about him, because there may still be a chance for Garret and me. A chance at what we had Before. A chance for our plans.

Mightn't there?

annie

That was me.
The girl with too many friends.
Some fake
some real.

annie

then i pay
good or bad
i know the answer
i show the answer

now i choose

annie

There's my sister walking in almost late.
Alone.
To her locker.
Right next to mine.
My heart clenches seeing her.
Have I ever loved
like she did?
(yes! Yes, I have!)
Like she still does?
Ever cared the way I saw
her care?
Know she cares?
(yes! Even more! I have!)
Ever planned more than a
scholarship from a glamour shot
and the correct answer of
World Peace?

sarah

I rush to my locker so I won't be late. Though the hall is crowded, I feel like a whispered word. I pass the offices and think of how there was so much arranging done when I started high school. All those people to help fix me.

I didn't think it was possible. But it helped. They helped me.

"A language," the guidance counselor had said as we prepared my ninth-grade schedule. "You need a language so you have all the right credits when you graduate."

Right! Me! A language! "One I don't have to speak," I said, trying to be funny.

"Got that," she said.

ASL. With Miss Saunders, the best teacher. Sign language, the best (and scariest) class I've taken.

A change from a lonely world to one that forces you to be watched by everyone. Could I go to a school that would train me in sign? Could I do Deaf Studies? Visit Gallaudet? That's what I decided to do by midterm my freshman year.

For years now, the schools we've attended have made sure Annie and I are separated and don't share classes. I think they've hoped I would "come out of my shell."

But it was sign language that changed me, if only for sixty minutes three times a week.

I love the noisy/soundless world of the deaf. The one place I am willing to stand out.

sarah

As I near Annie, who watches me come closer, I remember how on that first day of high school, I was terrified.

She waltzed into the building (like always). Everyone looked (like always). I followed. Watched people watch her. Did she even notice them? I was proud. Admiring her like everyone else did, feeling lucky because I was related.

Me, head tucked to my chest.

Her, head high, smile lighting up the hallway. She wasn't afraid, and so I followed her to where our lockers would be. Grateful to be with her. I let her open both of them. She spoke for me when teachers asked me anything, kept her arm around my waist when I started to panic, introduced me to the school — and to Garret that very first day.

"Hey, you look like you know what you're doing in math." She said that to him when she dropped me off in front of my Algebra classroom. I knew who he was. We'd seen him and his mom moving into the house on the corner. "Watch over my sister in there." She had stuck her hand out. "I'm Annie. This is Sarah. You're new to our neighborhood."

"Oh," he had said. "I'm Garret King." And I'd wanted to shake hands with him too, even though shaking hands is something that old people and beauty queens do.

sarah

I've gotten my books. Annie watches me, worried. She stands the way I do when I'm afraid. The way I do when I'm in an uncomfortable situation.

I see it then.

Is she waiting for me to notice?

Does she need me to see?

I'm not sure. We both reach for the paper at the same time. It's folded and stuck in the groove of her locker. Peeking out of that air vent.

sarah

Beauty Queen Pig. It says *beauty queen pig*.

Winter washes over me, like someone has left the hall door open. I swallow, swallow, swallow, but my throat stays dry.

Who?

Who?

The halls are flooded. Everyone is suspect. I look around. Turn in a circle. So many people hurrying past, but no one seems to wait for a reaction.

annie

Beauty
Queen

Pig

annie

Sarah rips the note to bits.
Grabs the words from my hands
and tears them to pieces.

"This is ..." She hesitates. Swears.
"They're wrong."
She sounds afraid.

But her eyes flick to my stomach.
She thinks it too,
thinks I'm a pig.

Her face goes bright red.
She thinks it too,
I'm sure.

annie

Her sister is a pig.
Yes.
I

 am.

annie

This is the way I want to be.
What I have decided to become.
I didn't know it at first.
Didn't see the power until the first few pounds
caused Mom to freak out.
My body knew I needed this
And I have gone along.
I have chosen to be fat.
Say it enough, the words are even more real.
Fat. Fat. Me.
These words are me.
And this is the way I want to be. This is the way I want to
be. This is the way I want to be.

This is the way.

annie

"Who?" Sarah says. "Who would do this?"
"Who would write these ... things?"
"Who would leave it here for you to find?"

She looks me in the eye and I can see she's going to cry.
"Why?"

I shrug.
There have been many, I want to say
Every day, I want to say
Sometimes more than once, I want to say.

"This," Sarah says, "is wrong
on so many levels."
She wipes at her tears.
"You don't deserve this."

I'm stunned.
Wait. I asked for this when I
Made my choice.
Still I say, "I don't?"

Sarah has a tight hold on my elbow.

"Who's doing it? Who's writing them?"

Guys I dumped?
Girls I stole boys from?
Beauty pageant competitors?

These could be from anyone
but I think I know.
"And, Annie, no. You don't
deserve these comments.
Ever."

"Not even if you think it too?" I ask.

"I don't believe it," she says.
And she's gone.
Back straight.
Hair swinging.
Not one sound from her
as she leaves.

I'm thinking.
I used to believe
I earned these notes
That I've been getting
         what I
         deserve

But maybe
I don't.

sarah

When we separate and head to class, I stop at the bathroom and weep in a stall for my sister. I'm quiet. Practiced. Flush the toilet if I have to sob. But I can cry without a sound if I have to.

"Who would do this? Who would want to hurt her?" I can't look at myself in the mirror. Refuse to step out of the stall at all. My voice is low but I can almost hear the echo of the questions.

The bell rings, and I don't care. I keep seeing Annie holding that note. And her face, it never changed. Each time I remember, I cry again.

When I know I can, I leave the bathroom for a late pass. I want to go home. Go find Annie. Make her take me home. Make her leave with me.

But Garret's waiting when I push into the hall.

I stumble with surprise, and he steps forward. There's no one else out here. Why isn't he in class? Did he hear me cry? Or did the buzz of voices from under closed classroom doors drown me out?

"What are you doing here?" I ask.

"I saw you and Annie."

I know my eyes are red. Lashes wet. Nose runny. But when I speak, I'm thrilled, broken, upset, delighted that I get to talk to him today. More than just the, "Hey, Sarahs." And the "Did you get the homework in American History?"

Annie says give us a break. To not think of Garret. She's right.
I know she is.

"So?"

"I could see you were upset. I've been waiting for you. What's
wrong?" he asks.

I have to look up to peer into his eyes. He's basketball tall
(though he plays rugby). His hair's a little longer than the last
time we were this close.

I love you.

Forget him.

I miss you.

Words get caught in my mouth, try to pass my teeth. *Pig* is in
there and *We're too serious* and that image of my sister looking so
afraid. I can't say any of that. Can't put words to those thoughts.
Nothing is full or spoken. I want to tell Garret everything — like
I used to — even though I shouldn't. Instead, I shake my head
because tears will spill if I speak, and I don't want him to think
those tears are for him. I may be heartbroken, but I have some
pride.

I manage to say, "I'm having an off day." A fluorescent light
above flickers, buzzes, goes out. The hall just-like-that feels like
a scene from a slasher movie. Garret says nothing, just steps
nearer — quiet, pretty the way he is, Garret. He wears that soft
leather jacket, the one that almost feels like satin. His hair is
damp — maybe from the snow? I lick my lips without meaning to.

"Need company?"

I don't answer.

I can do what Annie says.

So I walk. He goes down the hall with me and I am struck, like
a fist hits me, of walking down this very hall when Garret reached

for my hand, caught his fingers in mine. My face went red then and I lost my voice that day too.

This walking close is something I miss. The way his hand brushes mine. (On purpose? Not on purpose?) There's other stuff too. Like the fact that Garret is nice. How many guys out there are nice? (Did a guy write that note? A girl? Did Garret write the notes? Would he? Why? No. No, it was someone else.) I miss the way he laughs. Miss watching him play sports. Watching movies at my house. Doing homework at his. It all sort of crashes through my head, the memories. I'm so dumb. I shouldn't want to walk beside him. But I do. I should let him go, like Annie says. But today I can't.

I can't.

So even though I don't say anything and neither does Garret, we walk in step like we're meant to be together. Like we always did. The two of us. There's not a word between us. Just the sound of our feet on the tile floor.

sarah

At lunch, Annie finds me at my corner table and plops down next to me. She pulls out her food (homemade, of course). We could go home, but with weather like this, we'd never get back in time.

Three girls sit a few seats away. They whisper. Stare. One catches my eye. Lyndi, who was in a photography class with me last year, raises her eyebrows. It's like this every day. The queen has fallen. Is that what they think?

Does it bother Annie like it does me?

Am I making something of nothing?

When I glance back, they've pulled out *Norton's Anthology* and Lyndi thumbs through the pages.

I look away. A real sister, a true friend, would stand up, speak out, confront anyone who even seems to be acting nasty. But not me. I'm numb with anxiety. Did any of these girls leave that note?

The lunchroom is uncomfortable. I don't like being here. I used to eat in the library, where there wasn't the pounding noise, where the room wasn't crammed hot with bodies. Then the librarian said no more.

Today I didn't bring anything. Not even cash. I was too sick to my stomach. Somebody lets out a yodel. Another person has turned on music.

I put my hands on my stomach. Feel it move as I breathe. Concentrate on that — the air coming into my lungs. Leaving my body. Slow. Deep. No rushing or I might trigger a panic attack.

"You okay?" Annie asks.

I nod. Sure. Whatever.

A few tables over is where Melanie Simpson sits with Maeve Bradley and Georgie Wilde. Melanie has an empty chair beside her, and when she sees Annie, they wave at each other.

"Hey," Melanie says, calling over the din of voices. Her smile is genuine.

"Hey." And that's all from Annie.

I would never think, to see them talking like this (or not talking?), they used to be best friends.

"Have you been crying?" Annie asks when lunch is laid out before her. There's a turkey sandwich with avocado sticking out the edges, potato chips, a candy bar, banana, and Thermos with I-don't-know-what in it.

I look away and Annie moves closer.

"Why?" she asks. "Why, Sarah? Did someone say something to you? Or is this about Garret? Or that silly note?"

Garret walked me to class. Caught my wrist in his hand a moment then went on to Calculus. Bent close to me like he sometimes does when we see each other. Closer. Close enough I could put my arms around his neck. I won't. But I could.

I shake my head, clear my throat. Push at the nerves. "No. I'm okay." I'm a little louder this time, but not that much.

Annie offers me half her sandwich and I take it because I'm starved. Instant breakfast doesn't last long. Or maybe crying burns lots of calories.

Melanie talks loud enough for us to hear her (she's always

been loud. This group is loud. So was Annie.), but I don't listen. Many of Annie's friends from Before have filled in the chairs near us. They're laughing. Made up. Pretty.

Melanie waves to someone, and I see it's Garret. She's telling him to come over. Come here, Garret. Sit here.

I must have imagined his closeness earlier.

I'm shaking on the inside when I catch his eye. Then don't watch what happens. I'm not sure I can stand it if he stays with beautiful Melanie, my sister's used-to-be best friend.

"He's such a …" Annie stops talking.

"He doesn't owe me anything," I say. I know that. He can sit where he wants. With whomever he wants to sit. He plops into the chair near Melanie and she kisses his face hello like she's from Europe or something.

"You better not be crying because of him," Annie says. She looks at me, hard.

"No," I say. That kind of crying is for home. Not school. That kind of crying is embarrassing and can be loud and is mostly reserved for the shower or when I'm all alone in the house. And why isn't she weeping over that note? Why am I the one left to mourn over this?

Melanie laughs like she's read my thoughts.

"Good. Let's talk." Annie picks up a potato chip. Waves it in front of me. "I want." She pauses. "To start." She grins in my face. "A club." She points to my half of her sandwich. "I want it to be the kind that won't discriminate against people because of the way they look. Or how they think or even what they do."

How much did that note bother her? Does she remember the color of the ink? The slant of the letters? The hole where some-one pressed too hard on the paper?

It's so loud in here my ears hurt.

"You'd be perfect at that. Perfect." Annie is an expert at this kind of stuff. A pageant girl spends a lot of time doing community service. Organize things for the good of others.

Annie bounces in her seat. "I know, right?" She takes a bite of sandwich. Chews slow. She gestures at me with the avocado side of the bread. "You could help."

Out of the corner of my eye, I can almost see Garret. I pretend to pay attention to Annie.

"Want to?"

"How?" I sip at chocolate milk she's set in front of me, poured from the Thermos. There's a hint of malt in it. It's yummy.

"Could you make a few fliers in your design class?"

I look at my sister. Pause. Wait. Think it through. I could, with a little help from Mrs. Staheli. "Sure. What would you want?"

Annie hesitates. Then, with a gulp, she says, "What Mom said last night got to me." She sort of glances away, like she's embarrassed. "A mom always thinks her kid is beautiful. That's what I thought." She pauses. "Sarah, am I so fat I'm not pretty anymore?"

Now I'm listening with all of me.

Annie's inches from my face. Looking me right in the eye. Voice low.

A note from a stranger, bad enough. Stinging words from your mother? The worst.

You were pretty. You were.

When I answer, there's hurt in the words.

"You're beautiful, Annie," I say. And I mean it.

annie

This is me.
Safe.

The way any girl should be.

sarah

In design class I think, *A club?*
Is this something, could this be something I might be able to
do for Annie?

Adobe Photoshop is set up on my computer.

A flier is easy. Won't take much time at all. A good flier? That
will take a little thought. Maybe working on this will help Annie
and I become even closer. Cup-my-face-in-her-hands close.

The room is filled with the hum of talk as people work on different projects. Alex Henry sings under his breath. I stare at him, trying
to see if I know the song. It's something I've heard on the radio.
He looks up, sees me watching him. (Why am I watching him? My
skin goes sunburny.) Gives me a wave. His hair is cut short. When
he smiles, his eyes disappear in a squinty line. He has a nice mouth.

"Hey, Sarah," he says.

"Hey." I feel my face go red from embarrassment and pleasure.
Who would think I have room in my heart for a cute boy to make
me smile?

"What are you working on?" He walks over, dragging his chair
behind him.

"Ummm." There's that panic. The fear of speaking. The want-
to-run feeling.

Alex sits next to me. I feel his warmth. His knee touches mine.

The screen's blank.

I force myself to look at him even though, for a moment, I think that avocado sandwich might come back up.

"I don't have anything yet. But." Deep breath. I can do this. Get beyond sweaty palms. Come on! "I'm thinking of a slogan for a club."

"Club?" Alex's eyes are too blue to look at. He has a perfect smile. He looks at the blank screen with me.

"Kind of discrimination free. Be who you want to be." It's a wonder I don't stutter. "I'm helping my sister."

"Cool." He nods.

Does he know Annie? Of course he does.

I try to think of everything Mrs. Staheli has taught us. What are the best colors to use? The best words? What catches the eye?

"I can help out a little," Alex says. He's settling in. He smells so good. "If you want. I finished my project."

"Sure," I say, thankful I've spoken at all.

If helping Annie helps us, I'll try for her. I'll talk to Alex Henry.

Once I punched a neighborhood kid in the nose when he said Annie was ugly. Knocked him clean off his bike. That's what I want again. That kind of a relationship. Where I'm not scared to risk anything.

So Alex and I play around for a while. He suggests a sans-serif for the font. We decide on blue and gray as the palette. We move words. Phrases. Keeping it short and sweet, like Mrs. Staheli says. "People don't want to waste time reading when they're walking down a hall. Driving past a billboard. Keep it pithy."

We don't talk much.

But I catch Alex looking at me more than once. And when I do, he smiles, eyes disappearing, every time.

annie

A club for misfits.
A place to fit in.
Saying the word lets oxygen into my lungs
and I can breathe.

sarah

We show the work to Mrs. Staheli, Alex scooting closer so our teacher can see the screen better.

"You want the colors to pop. Try this." Mrs. Staheli makes a few small changes. "See?"

I nod.

"It's compelling, though a little dark. What do you think? And how many fliers will you want?"

Alex has his arm on the back of the chair.

How many? Will people even show up for Annie's club?

The Beauty Pageant Pig

"If Annie gets permission, I'd think several per hall," our teacher says when I don't answer. Then she rests her hand on my shoulder and says, "Good design, Sarah."

I sort of nod. "Alex helped."

Are these nerves for Annie or about getting so much attention from my teacher, or because Alex is moving his chair away, back to his own computer?

annie

I've been on the outside long enough now
to know who is here
at the edges.
I see them
alone
heads down, some
reading or studying the floor or focused on their hand-
held devices.

How do they feel
to not
fit in
when maybe they want to?

Do they hurt?
Pretend to be okay?
Nurse wounds at home
at school
or
alone?

How many of them are like Sarah?

annie

And
I have been on the other side
I have been the mean girl
I have hurt the loners —
the person I am now
the person I choose to be
the person my sister has always been

I have walked away from friends
from family
from truth
from myself.

Will I stay me
if I make a place
for all of us?

annie

My focus was so thin then. Narrow.
It's as if with my fat I have grown
a broader view of the world.
I am focused
on me yes now
but not like before.
Not on just the shiny parts of who I am.
But the beating parts too. The parts that
matter. The heart.

annie

I cannot go back and
make it all better.
Unhurt who I hurt.
Who I ignored.
Who I pushed out of my way.

I can't flush away
my own pain
the words of a note writer
a mother
a man
my own self

But if I can
help even a few
find hope
and if I help me too
then this will be a
part of my

redemption.

annie

Redemption.

Does it take the pain
move it far
narrow it to nothing?

Will the fear subside
shame leave
dark grow light?

Can I fix myself
get rid of the vile
push out the black

or
is this unseen part
of me
forever?

Am I married to my
ugly
secret?

sarah

I'm fresh from sign language class. Almost smiling while finger spelling my way down the hall. The day has evened out. I've calmed from the morning. From talking to my teacher and sitting so close to Alex. From agitating myself with thoughts and memories.

Ahead, I see Annie. She stands in line in front of the cheerleading squad, who are running a bake sale for new uniforms. Annie's coat hangs near her elbows, like a cape that slowed her to a stop in front of sweets. The hall is crowded, rumbling with noise, the floor wet from leftover snow on shoes, ringing with the sounds of lockers slammed shut. One of the male cheerleaders tries to do three back handsprings, but can get only two completed because so many people crowd the area.

It's almost too much stimulation for me. I want to clap my hands over my ears, but that kind of behavior isn't acceptable. I must tolerate, breathe through, calm myself in quiet ways.

So I watch my sister. Students pass like water around her. A few mill at the table, waiting to purchase goodies. Someone bumps into her, another kid speaks to her and she nods, flashing a smile at him. He cuts in line and buys something for himself.

All the while Annie studies the baked items. Brownies and cookies and cupcakes. All colors. She calls to me.

"Sarah, I see you," she says, even though she hasn't even looked in my direction. "Want something?"

Okay, truth be told, even on my worst days I can tell when she's near too. I know when she's snuck into my room late at night.

I concentrate on getting to Annie, block out the frenzy of the halls between classes, between the calls of the squad captain to buy for Springfield High spirit. When I'm close enough to really hear her, Annie says, "Did you come up with something spectacular?"

A couple of people glance at me and I feel my skin turn warm then cool off. I nod, move so we're shoulder to shoulder.

"I did," I say. "I sent it to you. You should be able to see it."

Annie flips through her phone, opens my text. Reads through and then looks at me, eyes sparkling. "Sarah, I love it."

"You do?" Her happiness thrills me. I grab Annie's hand and she squeezes my fingers. When I glance up, I can see us in the reflection of the office window. Can see the cheerleaders. Even the color of cupcake frosting in the glass. We're not broken apart like at home.

The crowd flows around and Tommy Jones (with a couple of jocks) calls out, "No more food, fat freak."

Annie doesn't react.

I do a double take. Have I heard wrong? But I know I haven't. My face burns. Down my neck. On my chest. I want to run after that kid and punch him in the throat. Knock him off his bike. If he had one, I mean.

Annie smiles, says, "I can't wait to see it printed."

For the first time in forever, I don't struggle to say anything. "I can show it to you later," I say. I'm talking too loud. "I'll get a hardcopy for you."

Melanie brushes near and says, "Hey, Sarah. Annie. Getting something for the team?"

Then she's off. Gone on down the hall with the crowd.

annie

fat
freak
ugly
you used to be
you were so
i remember when
stop eating
stop moving like that
you made me
you're responsible
not my fault
not another bite
don't wear that
don't show that
how could you
diet
pig
whale

sarah

O h." My voice travels down the hall, thin and high.
Side by side, in the reflection of glass, with the two of us together, I can see Annie's alone. Even with Melanie speaking in a kind way, even with me standing right here beside. I almost see Annie think the words.

Food is my friend.

Does she think I'm her friend too?

sarah

Tommy Jones still asks me to go out with him," Annie says. The hall is clearing. Annie buys a cupcake for me. Pale pink with silver sprinkles. One for her, dark chocolate with mocha icing.

"I didn't know that."

"He's been asking me out for more than a year."

He's in my sign class. His parents are deaf, I think, and he assists Miss Saunders by chatting with her so we can try to reverse interpret conversations.

I feel sick to my stomach. "I didn't know he was such a jerk."

Before it used to be the guys just showed up at the house. Annie knew they were coming, of course. But I never did. Sometimes, on Saturdays or Sundays, she might even go out with more than one guy. You know, one for lunch, another for dinner. But I haven't seen Annie go out with anyone for a while.

"Why's he so rude?" I want to say I hate him, but that's an immature response, so I just think it. Though I'll never look at him the same in class again.

"I won't go with him." She smiles at me. It's weird. Like fake. No warmth there. "Not my type."

Is she hurt by his words? Is she used to this name calling? Just like that, I'm sure he put that note in her locker. I know he did it.

A couple of freshmen come over to the table, one pulling money from her pocket. "I'll hurry," she says, "so we're not late."

"Go ahead of me," Annie says.

"Thanks," the girl with to-the-butt red hair says, "I have to have the one with M&M's." She speaks to Annie, who smiles at her. She hands over the money, takes a couple of M&M brownies, then both freshmen run off down the hall.

I watch them go.

"And his two buddies, the fullback and the safety?" Annie says, like the girls were never here. Three cheerleaders behind the table are all on their phones. One looks up every now and then to see if maybe we want to buy more.

The guys have headed in the opposite direction of the freshmen. I have no idea what she's talking about, but I nod anyway.

"They trapped me by the gym so Tommy could kiss me. Held me so I couldn't get away." Annie still has that smile on her face.

"Annie!" I raise my fingers to my lips. There's icing by my fingernail. "Are you serious?"

Her face goes red in two round spots. Like too much blush. Outside, the afternoon sky looks like almost-night. I feel sick to my stomach.

"Why didn't you tell me?" I touch Annie on the jacket, but of course she doesn't seem to notice.

She shrugs. "I took care of it. Screamed like nothing else and kicked him hard in his ..." She hesitates. "Manhood. Or lack thereof. Talked to someone at the office. All three of them were suspended."

I feel dizzy, like I've been spinning too long. "But ..."

How could I not know? I thought we were connected. Knew things about each other. Felt each other's pain.

"I didn't tell anyone at home. I spoke up at the office only because the principal said she wouldn't tell you all."

"You should have told me."

But it's like Annie doesn't hear me. "You understand, Sarah," she says, peeling the cupcake wrapper free and dropping it in the garbage can. We ease toward the science wing, where I know she has Earth Sciences. "This weight is something I choose."

"Did you ever tell Mom or Dad?" The cupcake feels too heavy. Like it gained weight sitting in my hand.

I should tell. Right now. Text our parents. But I feel helpless all the way to my fingertips. "When?"

"Doesn't matter now."

"It does matter, Annie." There's a pain building behind my eyes.

"I made a formal complaint," she says. "And Mom and Dad found out. Didn't matter that I said not to tell anyone. Jones was suspended, and he'll never bother me again."

"Not physically, you mean," I say. "But he called you ... he said those awful ... words."

She nibbles at the edge of the cupcake. Eats off a bit of icing. This is delicate eating. Not the kind of intake that makes someone gain so much weight the way she has. "And I think he's doing the notes. Pretty sure of it."

I nod. I am right.

People holler, and my head hurts like I've held my breath too long. There's an announcement over the intercom for teachers to turn in midterm grades by four p.m.

An adult coming in from outside bumps into me, says nothing, and continues on down the hall like I'm not here. And when I look into the glass for my reflection, I see it's gone, like I've disappeared with Annie's confession.

sarah

Melanie, Alison, Maeve, Emily, Georgia, Taylor, Brooklyn. And Annie.

Not one of the girls who used to come to our house to do their hair and makeup, who would pose this way and that, who tried on their dresses then promenaded down the stairs, crowns on heads held high — not one of them visits Annie anymore.

Her weight gain has changed so much for her.

But not chased the horrible guys away.

Those girls and her, they used to walk like something from a movie, in two lines. Annie leading the pack. Now she roams the hall alone — I'm beginning to wonder if this choice is hers.

Like me.

But different.

Of course, different.

She talks to people, yes. Makes pleasant conversation. She talks to someone now, as she leaves me there in the hall. But then she moves off and walks solo. Her back straight, her head high, like one of her tiaras is still there.

sarah

It's freezing outside. I've come to the car to warm it, and I'm waiting for Annie, watching people pass. I know lots of these kids from Before, when my sister was thin and chose to be popular.

No one speaks to me. No one waves at me. Notices me in the car. And just like that, I know why.

"I'm responsible," I say out loud. "For this. For being alone." I roll the words around on my tongue. Taste them. Think about how I have, as Mom would say, made my bed.

My never talking to anyone, never answering in class, having few friends, has made me just what I wanted to be — invisible. For a moment the thought is unnerving.

This is the place I have settled, I realize, as I wait while listening to Bach. This is the place I feel comfortable. Maybe like Annie, used-to-be-thin Annie, and her fat?

Do I like it?

Yes. And no. I would rather not be so afraid. I've been afraid since third grade. And since third grade, I've been doing what I can to be alone.

"It'll get better," people said. A therapist. Neighbors. Extended family. "Give her time."

"Well," I say, hands clasped in my lap, people walking past. "I've done it. I've succeeded."

Am I proud of who I've become?

Melanie leaves the building, skipping through the parking lot, flashing past our car. She slips on ice. I watch to see if she might fall. Hope she will.

She doesn't.

The sun tries to pierce the heavy clouds. Breaks through with watery light. The Sirius Radio announcer talks about the piece just played. The windows fog up.

Can I change who I am? Fight the panic? Do what Mom's always wanted?

Melanie walks over to a girl I know is on student council. I turn on the seat warmers. Close my eyes. Wonder.

Is Melanie dating Garret? I've only seen them in the lunchroom. A little around school, nothing more. No more hints than her European air kisses.

Does he like her? Think of her?

I want to know. I don't want to know. Why do I care?

Is he with someone else? Someone I don't know?

Does Garret King remember our moments together?

I gaze at the sun that's weak and giving up the battle with the afternoon storm pushing toward us.

Alex Henry pops into my head and I blush.

Is his mom like Garret's?

Oh the breaking up.

I've not told anyone. Have hardly let myself think of it.

I try to settle in the car. Try to stop my face from heating up from the event.

She told him to take it easy and so he did.

She said we were kissing too much, spending too much time together wrapped in each other's arms. She told him to cool it. I blamed her for the first few weeks.

But Garret listened.

"I'm a single mother," she said. "I don't want to end up a single grandmother. I've made our money, and I don't plan on sharing with a girl who gets pregnant too young."

"We haven't done anything wrong," I said when he told me. "We never had sex."

Garret looked away. We were on my front porch, and when he peered in the direction of his house I got the uncomfortable feeling that maybe his mother watched us.

"I told her that," Garret said. "But she wants me to keep dating."

"We are," I said. "We are dating."

He looked at his hands then. "Dating other people," he said. "Seeing who else is out there."

He couldn't tell me why. But I knew the reason. Somehow, I wasn't good enough.

The sky is darker now. Pewter.

Maybe it wasn't me.

Maybe it was her.

Maybe, maybe he just didn't stand up to her and let her know how he felt.

By the time Annie is opening the car door, I wonder if maybe Garret and I loved each other too fast, too hard.

sarah

Dad stops me and Annie when we come in from school and asks us to be sure to have a musical number prepared for Saturday night.

"Sure," Annie says.

I say nothing. Feel my mouth go dry. Some irony that I'm wondering if I want solitude and then Dad asks us this.

My violin brings me great joy.

When I hit that high note, perfect a song, press my chin into the rest and hold the bow like it's a part of me.

But playing for Dad's party makes my afternoon cupcake feel like a chunk of ice.

I hurry up the stairs, giving no answer to my father. And once in my room, I decide to take Annie's suggestion to heart. I'll not stay stuck in my ex-boyfriend's memories. I'll be a free woman.

My room is dark and cool, and I hear the murmurs of Mom talking to Dad somewhere downstairs.

The shade's drawn so I can't see his house, and down the hall, Annie's singing. She has an awful voice, but she doesn't care. She belts out old-timey show tunes at the top of her lungs. I have to smile.

This room is filled with Garret mementoes. I decide I can break away. I can do it a bit at a time. And I can start here.

I set to gathering all the stuff that reminds me of him. His sweatshirt I kept one night when he walked me home in the rain. The shoebox filled with handwritten notes he stuck in my locker last year, sometimes two or three a day. (Sweet notes. Make-me-blush notes. Not like what Annie got.) The collage of photos of us I stuck up around my mirror, on a corkboard, on the closet door. So many photos of us, happy in every one.

I pack everything in a box that I tape shut and put on the top shelf of my walk-in closet. When it doesn't hurt so much to try to stop caring, I'll throw it away.

Then I wander to my window and let the shade up, exhausted. Who knew feeling could do this to a person. Wear them out. Break them up. I fall onto my bed and cry for a good half hour into my pillow, because this is the end.

annie

Has Sarah heard me cry?
The late nights
in the showers
in my closet?

I hear her now.

Weeping.

I stand at her door
and listen.
Does she need me
or will this cry
set her

free?

sarah

When I am cried out, when my nose is stuffy and my eyes swollen, I lie on my back in bed and remember. A sort of final thinking — intentional remembering — like at a funeral when people talk of their best memories of the one who's died.

The last time Garret was in this room the aurora borealis colored the sky. A phenomenon, Dad said earlier when we all went to stare at the view. Garret snuck in late by climbing up on the roof and into my window like Romeo had for Juliet.

I greeted him with a kiss, my arms around his neck. Not one bit of shy at all. We'd talked, lying in my bed on top of the covers, then I'd slept snuggled against him till his phone woke us. It was three a.m. by then, and it was his mom calling, wondering where he was and then, believe it or not, a few minutes later my mom knocked on the door.

"Sarah? Sarah? Why is the door locked?"

Garret didn't have time to do anything more than fall to the floor.

"I'm sleeping, Mom," I'd said, but I'd opened the door still wearing the clothes I'd had on that day. Not realizing until it was too late.

Mom looked me up and down. She said, "What's up?"

Dim light fell in from I-don't-know-where and the window

screen was right there against the wall, and my boyfriend lay on the floor, sort of hidden. Nervous laughter filled my throat. There were so many clues.

"Annabelle King is on the phone." Mom stood there. Her hair looked like she'd run a brush through it. How? When I wake up, I wonder if rats have made nests.

"Why?" I blurted the word out.

"You tell me," Mom said.

We stared at each other.

"You woke me." The almost truth.

She nodded. Turned and headed off down the hall, waving her hand at me. "That better be all," she'd said. "And that woman better not call here again."

I closed the door, on fire for so many reasons, and Garret sat up. "Doesn't sound like your mom likes my mom very much."

I shrugged, then fell across the bed, kissing him as he sat there, putting my hands on his face. He tasted like spearmint, even this late at night. I kissed him once more out the window, leaning onto the roof to murmur my goodbye.

We did that a lot. Spent the nights together. Talking. Dreaming. Kissing.

If I'd slept with him, if he had asked, if we hadn't decided early on we'd wait until marriage, would he have stayed? No matter what his mother said?

annie

In my drawer I hide essentials.
       Things to get me through the night
If I cannot sleep.
         Snickerskitkatsm&m'srolosbighunks
      Lay'spotatochipsgrandma'schocolatechipcookies-
              jalepeñocheeto's
Gummywormschocolatecoveredcinnamonbearsseafoam
        Doubledippedchocolatealmondstwizzlers
       skittlesstarburstsreecespeanutbuttercups
My secrets.

When the dream comes
      sometimes
I wake up eating
      Eating
in my sleep.

annie

he stands at the foot of the bed
the ghost
I
recognize

sarah

Girls," Mom calls. "I need help with dinner."

I take a deep breath, meet my sister in the hall, who hugs me (!!!), and we go downstairs to cook.

"Oh, Annie, have you ..." Mom says when we come into the kitchen.

I feel Annie tense up next to me.

Mom pauses. When she talks it's like she's in pain. "That outfit is not becoming at all." The room seems to go darker, even though outside the storm slides past with a rainy slush. So weird how Mom notices this one thing. Not that I've been crying or that I didn't come out of my room after we talked with Dad or that I'm feeling sad.

Now the late afternoon sun shines on the snow and tries to slip into this part of the house.

Our mother hands me the makings for a salad. I don't have to hide my eyes because she's doesn't look at me. She shakes her head. Tsks.

"When our guests arrive, you make sure to put on a black dress," she says to my sister. "It's slimming. I can't believe how much we still have to do. You know Daddy's clients are coming in from the city for a couple of days. You know we have to be ready."

"I'll be ready," Annie says. Cold like outside.

But Mom doesn't seem to hear. She has her head down. Pulls plates from the cabinets. Grabs silverware. She is not happy.

I want to say, "What does a black dress have to do with anything?" but I don't get the chance because Mom says, "Not too many onions, Sarah." She doesn't wait for my, "Yes ma'am."

And she doesn't see Annie give her the finger.

sarah

Annie's in her room. Door shut.
I jiggle the handle. Knock.

"I can talk to you about the flier now," I say, keeping my voice low. I rest my cheek on the door. It's cool. The paint smooth. "If you want to see it, Annie, I printed a copy downstairs."

My sister stays silent.

annie

Private time is not
What it used to be.

When I got the beginnings of breasts
(long before Sarah)
I stopped going shirtless
even though my sister
teased me.

When I got my period (two years before Sarah)
I was over
sharing a bed with her and
letting her walk in on me while I was bathing and
even done letting her borrow my clothing.

I closed up in this world of
Changing body
Admired myself
Curled my hair
Whitened my teeth
All while Sarah stayed a little girl
And I became a woman.

Now
Now I don't want this privacy
Though I lock my door
hide my journal
say to myself that it will be okay.

I want my mother to ask
what's wrong?
Not mention my dress size
or say I'm bigger
or unbecoming

I want my sister to snuggle me close.
Want my father to
find the bad guys and stop them.
I have kept my family away for so long that
they cannot see my distress
so I must defend me.

sarah

It looks good, that flier. And the assistant principal said this kind of club is a terrific idea.

Consideration. Judgment Free. Everyone Welcome.

Date.

Time.

Room number.

A faded face behind it all. Words where eyes should be. Where the mouth and nose should be.

I was scared to death to show it to Ms. Cleland. But Mrs. Staheli said I'd need to or Annie would, and after yesterday's closed door, I wasn't sure she would do it. Mrs. Staheli looked at me like I shouldn't be worried to talk to anyone in the office.

Out the door I went when the bell rang. Making my way, slow as I could without seeming like a weirdo.

And then it happened. Me standing in the hall, trying to calm my nerves. People racing. Passing me like ants going around a rock. The office was ten steps away by then and I was giving myself a pep talk. Ms. Cleland appeared, like magic, in the doorway.

"Walk forward," I said. "Take a step."

I forced my body to move. Stepped in the path of a train. Someone running straight into me. The flier crunched in my hands. His books went flying.

"Sorry. Sorry," I said. "Sorry."

Ms. Cleland helped the boy gather his books. "That was some hit, Jackson," she said, laughter in her voice. "And you, Sarah. Are you okay?" She offered to help me to my feet, but I ignored her. The floor was damp. Gritty. I stood. My ears rang. My shoulder ached. "I didn't see him." And ouch, I'd bitten my tongue.

"I saw that."

Then I handed the paper to her. "I ... I wanted to give this to you? For approval? To see what you think?"

I'm glad that meeting Ms. Cleland (in the hall, not even planned, even though there was a huge wreck) is over. My heart pounded for more than half an hour after the fiasco. But the neck ache was worth it for Annie.

sarah

I'm not sure why my getting approval for Annie's club makes me remember last summer and when she was madder than anything. Is it that she was a different kind of pain in the neck for me then? That she caused me real grief? The family too?

No. It's that I think summer is when I really saw a big change. The moment when things began to fall apart. And my wanting to help her now brings back the memory.

At the time, I had no idea what was going on with Annie. Why she felt so angry. Why some days she was happy, giddy-in-love happy about some guy, and then all-of-the-sudden furious. The back and forth made me dizzy.

This was a fury time.

She bit everyone's heads off for at least a week. Slammed doors. And when she didn't show up for work, Mom had to run me in to take my sister's place at Dad's office.

"That Annie," Mom had said, and we hurried to the city proper. She wore lipstick and there were dark circles under her eyes. "What are we going to do with her?"

And it wasn't like on TV where the mom is pretending to be sad or worried but is really happy, really proud and just wondering for the sake of some script. No. This was the real deal. A real question. Real heartbreak.

The whole way to work I'd said, "I don't want to do it, Mom. Please. Not the front desk. I can't."

And Mom repeated, "What am I going to do with her? What?"

I sweat handprints onto my shorts. Smelled of BO. Could have cried our whole way to drop me off (I did cry, later in the bathroom. Several times.).

Looking back at it now, I have to wonder what it was like for our parents to have one daughter who hardly spoke and another who ran her mouth all the time. They wore two expressions. There was the one with me, the can't-you-grow-out-of-this pose. The new look for Annie was to cringe anytime she came into the room. Who would she be today? What might she say or do next?

"I don't want to work the front desk," I said when we pulled into the real estate office parking lot.

Mom stared at me. Frazzled? Maybe. I bet she hadn't heard a word I'd spoken.

Our lives were twisting then, going this way and that. Annie was growing bigger. Heavier. And what Mom and Dad had taught us was normal — beauty queen, terrific college material, scholarships — seemed out of reach for her. She wasn't their normal anymore.

Usually Annie worked for Dad in the front lobby. Dressed up, complete with high heels. I only helped when Dad needed an extra hand, filing important paperwork. I kept to the back of the building, out of sight.

"I don't like to be where people are," I said, opening the car door. "Please."

The sun was too bright. The jean shorts I had on, and the nice top, were too hot. Too tight.

"I don't want to hear it," Mom said. She looked away from me. "And it'd be nice if you'd get a learner's permit."

I didn't answer. There was no way I was driving. I closed the door, and when I got to the office, Dad was waiting.

"Where have you been?" He didn't yell. But his words were rocks.

"I feel sick." And I did. It was no lie. I wanted to throw up. "Daddy …"

"Just answer the phone, Sarah, and take messages," Dad said. "I'm in a terrible bind." He was all dressed up. "What's so hard about that?" He looked at me, checked his watch, and shaking his head, took off down the hall. Another meeting and no competent daughter to secretary for him.

That day I sat at the desk, trembling. Vomit edged up the back of my throat. Tears filled my eyes, and I had to keep wiping them on my shirt. I wanted to run home.

Where was Annie? I should go where she'd gone.

I stared at pictures of three guys I thought she was going out with at the time. She had taped the photos to the shelf, eye-level.

The whole office wandered by. Bringing notes for me for when certain people called. Reminding me of their phone numbers. Asking where Annie was.

David came by speaking baby talk on his cell to one of his kids. "Hey," David said, covering the mouthpiece. "You're looking pretty, Sarah."

I fake smiled.

He put his elbows on the desk. Rested his chin on one hand. Took a Jolly Rancher from the jar between us.

"Where's your sister?" he asked. "I'm talking to Van, and he loves her."

I shrugged. Waited for him to leave. Hoped the office phone wouldn't ring.

Emma Jean hurried up from the back. She wore a dark suit and her hair was pulled up in a way Mom always said was most unbecoming. "She's had tons of cosmetic work done," Mom said. "Her face. Her body."

Dad said Emma Jean helped seal the deal on more than her fair share of houses, so he didn't care what she did cosmetically, and by the way, he thought she looked terrific. I handed Emma Jean a stack of manila folders, some several inches thick.

"Covering for that sister of yours?" Emma Jean asked.

What kind of question was that? One I didn't need to answer. But Emma Jean stood there. Waited.

"Yes," I said.

She nodded and left.

No wonder people bought houses from her. They were afraid not to.

Two of the boys in Annie's pictures I recognized from school. Had she met the other one on the Internet? Here? At a party?

The phone startled me when it rang. I told the person everyone was in a meeting, could I take a number? Sweat rolled down my back. I hung up.

About eleven thirty, Paul wandered in. He's older than Dad. They started this real estate company together, Paul using Dad's ideas, Dad using Paul's money.

Paul saluted me. Something green was stuck between his front teeth. He looked at me so hard that I felt uncomfortable. And then he said, "Sarah." His eyes were too blue—for an old man, I mean.

"What?" I'd almost yelled at him.

"Where's that looker of a sister?"

I flinched. Shrugged. Wasn't that sexual harassment or something?

The whole day was stressful and long. I stayed late with Dad because he said so, because Annie did sometimes, and then, at long last, the two of us drove home, Dad talking business the whole way.

I didn't listen. I just wanted to get in my room. Lie on the bed. Text Garret. Do anything to unwind. Every muscle in my body was taut.

My room. My room. That's what I thought running up the stairs. I slammed the door behind me and collapsed against it.

I fell on the bed, sweaty from nerves. Closed my eyes. Did the deep breathing that hadn't worked all day. Thirty minutes later, my heart had calmed down and my head no longer ached. I was changing my clothes when I heard, "What's your problem?"

Dad. Shouting. "Are you crazy? You must be. How can you do your runway walk like that?"

Uh oh.

The calm I had felt was shoved aside. I felt cold at Dad's words. Now what? A spasm of worry similar to what Mom might have been feeling earlier that day when Annie simply didn't show up for work coursed through me. Why hadn't I paid more attention to my mom? Tried to ease the way she felt?

I headed down the stairs unsure of where to put my feet, like I might step wrong and fall face-first into the foyer. Fights, yelling, anger. It all unnerved me.

Hesitating, I waited on the Persian rug in the foyer, listening to Dad. Taking in his anger. Hearing the heartbreak in his voice.

I was afraid to see why he sounded like this. His sorrow scared me. This was serious. And Annie was silent. I almost didn't allow myself to peek.

Dad hollered. Said, "What? Why?"

In the background, I could hear Mom weeping.

I looked into the living room, white as heaven. My father and sister stood toe to toe, squaring off. Mom sat in the corner, perched on a chair, her face covered with her hands.

Annie's hair was nearly gone.

It was as if she'd cut it raggedy short with a butter knife. She'd colored it purple, red, black. What was left of her hair looked bruised.

Our father was right. This was not a beauty queen's haircut.

Annie stood there so stiff, so small looking, so defiant. She argued, "My life" and "My hair." Then she said, "I wanted it this way."

Dad went silent. Took in a breath. "You're fired," he said. And that was that.

sarah

Not that much more before, a few months before the hair-cut, before Annie started gaining weight, Mom and Dad and I sat in an audience of more than three hundred people. Dad had invited his whole office. Paul and Emma Jean and David were there, with their families. Everyone wore an Annie: Queen of the Night T-shirt to support her. (She played that aria on the piano.)

My parents clapped like crazy when she won Miss Springfield and won a scholarship to boot. She dipped her head to accept a glittery crown. Her face was bright. She didn't cry like some winners do, but pumped her fist in the air. Laughed. Yelled into the microphone, "Mom! Dad! Sarah! I love you!"

Melanie was runner up. She laughed too. Grabbed Annie in a huge hug, and they almost danced. Then Annie waved to all those people like she meant it.

"Look at her," Dad said. "That's my girl."

"Our girl," Mom said.

"You could be a winner too, Sarah," Dad said. Then he was cheering for Annie again.

I was hot with emotion. Thrilled for Annie. But burning from the inside out. Had my dad really said that? We both knew I'd never stand on a stage like that. Ever. No matter what Dad said, I couldn't do what Annie did.

I didn't want to.

No matter how much he wanted me to be like Annie, I was just Sarah.

sarah

Here's what I'm thinking," Annie says. We're in the family room after dinner, a fire roaring in the fireplace. "Mom? Sarah?"

Dad keeps checking his phone. After the haircut, he quit looking at Annie when she spoke. When she pierced one of her ears in numerous places, he didn't talk to her for a week. When she pierced her nose, I thought he might collapse from anger. I think he doesn't look at her straight on anymore because he's afraid something new has happened.

Mom's watching *The Bachelor*. A long-ago season, and I'm not sure why she's turned it on now. She knows the outcome.

Mom pauses the show.

Annie's animated. Her eyes are bright. Liquid looking. Like what she plans to say means as much to her as that night on the stage last year. She glances at me.

Is she nervous? My sister the star. Is she afraid? Has she become like me because of her choices? Because of her weight?

"Mom, me and Sarah are starting a club," Annie says.

What? Me? No, not me.

Mom looks from Annie to me and back to my sister. She wears a tentative expression. Like she can't believe this. I don't blame her. "A club?"

"At school. Sarah got permission, of course, and I've spoken to Ms. Cleland too—you've met her, Mom, remember? With the incident?—and she said a diversity club sounds good to her."

My stomach drops at the allusion to Tommy Jones, but Mom nods. She wears a timid smile, like she's not quite sure what to do with her lips. Like when I'm in front of a class and I'm not sure where to put my hands. Am I my mother too? The thought surprises me.

"Is that so?" she asks.

Dad waves a hand, meaning shush. "This is about a meeting before the party," he says, then stands and says, "Gotta take this call."

"Tell me more, dear," Mom says, and for a minute she sounds like someone in a Lifetime movie. She sounds … fake. Does Annie notice? The nerves tighten.

How have we gotten so far from each other? Mom passes me the bowl of caramel popcorn she holds. It smells buttery. Sugary. I take a handful but Annie shakes her head no.

"I don't care who shows," Annie says. She sits close to Mom. Her voice is lowered. "Anyone can come. There's no judgment."

Mom nods. Dad moves across the room, stands near the fireplace here in the TV room. He's speaking low. The flames lick the air. The firewood snaps.

"So if you feel different, if your hair isn't quite perfect" — she reaches for her own hair — "if your nose is too big …" Annie has raised her voice. Does she want Dad to hear?

I'm quiet. Listening. Eating popcorn.

Hoping.

For what? I don't even know.

Mom's listening too. I can tell. She moves closer. "Annie."

"Sarah made a terrific flier." Annie looks at me and I raise my eyebrows. "And we'll hang them up everywhere." Then Annie starts listing flaws again. Are you the wrong color? The wrong religion? The wrong shape? The wrong class? The wrong age? The wrong … It just keeps going on and on.

Mom's hand goes to her throat.

I recognize the move. Have seen it when I couldn't talk at an assembly. When I walked out on a violin solo. When I didn't stand up to a bully in sixth grade. Mom is always touching her throat like she has to hold her head on.

"Are you sure you should associate with those kinds of people?" Mom asks, and the whole room goes quiet. Even Dad looks over like he can't believe Mom has spoken those words. Can he hear us?

Then Mom is up, moving out of her comfy chair, grabbing the popcorn and taking it with her.

My lungs are full of fire ants.

Annie's hands are folded in her lap and she doesn't change position. She tilts her head The two of us wait, together. Mom works in the kitchen. There's the clatter of cabinet doors shutting.

"With the lower class," Annie says after a long moment.

"She didn't mean that," I say.

"Yes, she did." Then Annie leaves the room.

I have to breathe through my mouth. Close my eyes. Under my hands I feel the texture of the sofa. It's a pale red, the leather, and soft.

Dad's voice seems loud now.

He's not paying attention. Maybe he never was. I stand. Walk into the kitchen. It seems so far.

Mom gazes out the window over the sink. The room is so bright there's no way she can see outside — the window shows only her reflection, then mine. Mom gasps and says, "You surprised me, Sarah."

Nothing from me.

"What?" she says. "Spit it out."

I swallow. I'm shaking. "I can't believe you said that to Annie, Mom."

She turns on the sink water. "What are you talking about?"

"We're not royalty."

The water runs in the sink. Dad's voice is a murmur in the background.

"I know that." Mom gives a ruffled laugh.

"It was mean. You were mean to her. She has a good idea that could help other people. Maybe help herself. And me."

"I don't know what you're talking about." The Lifetime movie is back. The front door opens. Slams shut.

"Great," Mom says. "Now we have to go after her, Sarah."

Like Annie is a bother.

Or the second-class citizen Mom's worried my sister will become.

annie

These are the rules:
Be who you are
Say what you will
Live your life well
You are safe here.

annie

Safe.

Here.

sarah

Annie's down the sidewalk, coatless, hands shoved into her pockets.

Mom speaks from the porch. Her words puncture the night air. "I don't want you hurt," she says. "But … those kinds of people, that kind of influence … It's not good for you."

"Stop talking, Mom," I say. Part of me is surprised I've said anything more to her. That I've talked back. But she doesn't answer, so I follow Annie, leaving my coat behind too, but grabbing mittens and a scarf from the foyer table where I left them when I came in this afternoon. I pull the gloves on. Wrap the scarf around my neck.

"Annie!"

The blast of winter hits me full in the face, makes me gasp, and I'm reminded of Garret. Maybe because I can see the lights on over there, see his car parked in his driveway.

For two weeks, before we started dating, he took me to school.

Annie had decided she wouldn't finish out a term, but would home school.

And Mom needed me to catch a ride into classes. Garret happened to be available.

The cold bites at me, the wind pushes me back like a hand.

Mom's talking, talking, talking and then the door slams shut and I remember how Garret'd knocked on the door, walked me to the car, opened that door. Big Gulp cups. Everywhere. Front seat. Backseat too.

"What is all this?" I had said.

"My collection," he had answered.

Now I can see my breath. There's Annie, jogging in the opposite direction of my used-to-be boyfriend's house. So much of our lives, I realize as I follow her, is used to be's.

I run, purposefully sliding on the ice I see, hitting as much snow as I can so I don't fall.

Here's how I felt about Garret, from the beginning: I'm pretty darn neat as a rule, but I settled myself in that car, kicking the cups out of the way, without a thought.

The memory makes me warm inside, even with tonight's low temps. I hurry through the cold. The sidewalk is slicker than I'd thought.

Oh, I liked him. That morning he'd popped his toothbrush in his mouth and brushed all the way to school. The car smelled minty fresh but looked like a dump.

"Good dental habits?" I'd said. It took all my courage. My face caught fire.

Garret smiled.

I surprised myself then too. Me, shy. But his teeth were white. Did he floss? I hoped so. But I'd hoped he wouldn't do that while we drove.

My mouth opened before my brain had a chance to stop it. "You have a great smile." I spoke like a real person.

Garret glanced at me. "What was that?"

"Nothing," I had said, almost stuttering.

It wasn't long after that he asked me to the movies. Oh, that car! He was cute and I hadn't minded the Big Gulp cups at all.

I'm right behind Annie now. She must hear me because she turns, spinning. I put my hands up, like she might strike out. But she walks into my arms and we stand in the cold, shivering, freezing it seems, holding each other. I wrap the scarf half around her, half around me. I give her one glove and we hold bare hands.

"She doesn't mean it," I say. I say this too much. Always protecting her. Them. Annie. When did this become my job? "I'm not sure what's wrong with her." With them, I think. With us. "But she's trying in her weird way."

I believe what I say, I realize, as the words tumble out and hit the sidewalk.

Annie's teeth chatter. "She means every word." Annie blows out a cloud of air and it floats above her head like a word bubble. "I started this all. This family change. I realized that when she was talking. My deciding to gain weight, to drown in food, it's changed everything."

The wind pushes at us. Her words push at me. A car drives past, snow crunching under tires. Annie stares into my eyes.

"They've always been like that," I say. "Money matters. The way we look to others." I clutch her ungloved hand in mine. My fingers have gone numb, though my palm is still warm. "But underneath the fake crap, they care. She cares. She's just …" I reach for words. "Shallow, and she can't crawl up from that."

The wind whips my hair. Pushes me and Annie closer.

"We used to matter more," Annie says. "Before this." She doesn't gesture or anything, but I understand what she means. "Before, we mattered."

I don't answer.

"What?"

A dog barks. One long, low howl. A door opens and shuts somewhere.

"Not we," I say.

"Tell me. Say it."

"You've always mattered more."

annie

She's right. Yes.
I know it.
As we walk
hand in hand
I'm so embarrassed
at this truth.
The scarf around
neither neck fully.
One glove each.
Sarah is right.
Mom and Dad showed
They loved me
more than her.
And I'm sick
with this revelation
I had hoped
she didn't know.

annie

After our mother's stupid comments
and Sarah's announcement of feeling unloved
I decide I am done with all this.
The being overweight.
The clutching of secrets.
The listening to my parents, who sound like idiots.

But I am done on my own terms.
My.
Own.

sarah

This is what they said: "Sarah, try smiling. Do it like Annie."
Walk like her. Laugh like her. Succeed like her.

I heard it from her friends: "You two are related? Sisters? Twins?"

And from teachers: "I never would have known the two of you are just minutes apart in age."

Dad's coworkers: "That Annie is something else. And Sarah. Sarah is a shy little thing, isn't she?"

From everyone except Garret.

Once, when we were at school, Annie came flitting up to Garret and me. She was happy about a date that night. Something secret and exciting, she said. Then she was off with Melanie and the rest of the girls.

"I like your sister," Garret said as we watched her go. Then he reached over and kissed me. Right there in front of everyone. "But I am so glad you're you."

sarah

And I was glad to be me when I was with Garret. Maybe that's why it hurts so much to be alone. Is it even possible to let people know the Invisible Girl is an okay person?

annie

After lights out
I gather the candy
lay it out on the blanket
and eat
till I want to throw
up.

sarah

I'm sleeping when Annie comes into my room. She's quiet as a shadow. But I wake when I hear the door click shut. It takes a moment for me to realize what's going on. That she isn't sleep-walking or coming to borrow something to wear tomorrow.

She moves like smoke through the room, looks out my window, checks the latch. I don't say anything. Just lie there.

Annie checks the closet, looks under the bed. Quiet as a whisper she says, "I'm watching for you, Sarah. That's what older sisters do. Take care of the babies."

The baby? I almost say it.

Then her words sink into me.

I'm cold with what she's said. Like when we stood outside tonight. But this fear is in my chest. Who's she looking for? How am I a baby?

Annie stays in my room, waiting on the chair at my desk until I sleep again.

annie

If your mother doesn't protect you
      you have to do it yourself.
That's what I have found.
         Found you can't always rely on the people
            you should be able to rely on.

Like your father.
      Your father should know better.
            So it's better than nothing that I check
                  on Sarah and I have been checking
for months now.

No one else does.
No one else will.

I'm scared.
      Scared of what I can do.
            Of what someone else might do.
      Scared for my sister.
            For me.

         For me.

annie

Up close.
Too close.
I feel his breath.
His hands.
How he wants me.
The pressure.
I awake with a start.

wednesday

sarah

In the morning, I catch Annie in the bathroom we share. I think of her in my room last night. Was it a dream?

My hand is on the doorknob. It's cool under my fingertips. No. She was there.

Annie's sat in my room while I slept before. It's just never felt so odd.

That chilly feeling is back.

My sister leans close to the mirror, peering at herself from all angles. She's showered, wearing her towel tucked around her chest. There's no black eye makeup. Her hair is slicked back. The earrings glitter. Annie purses her lips, pouts, gives herself a sultry stare.

As I back from the room, leaving her to the mirror modeling, she says, "Hey, Sarah" in this voice like pudding.

"Oh!" I'm embarrassed, like I was caught posing.

"You can stay if you want." Annie turns to me. Adjusts the towel. Her toenails are a shiny pink. Pink? They've been black for months now. "I want you to. We can talk." She hesitates. "Do you want to talk?"

I step onto the warm tile. The orange-y odor of the soap Mom buys from Milton's Herb Shop scents the room.

"Yes," I say. "I do." I turn on the water and wet my face.

This bathroom is all our mom, from the pink-and-white wall-paper to the matching pink towels with satin edging. Everything reflects in the mirrors.

When I've dried my face, I brush my teeth then add a touch of conditioner through my hair, taming the curls.

"Annie?"

"Hmmmm?"

"Last night?" I try to think how to say this. "Who were you watching for?"

My sister pauses. Glances at me, side-eyed. "I've been checking on you since you were little," she says. "When we shared a bed, I sat up late, watching over you."

I don't respond.

Does she know about Garret in my room after hours?

She wouldn't look for him. Would she? This was something else. Something scary.

"Since we were little?" I say.

She's taken black liner to her eyes. But she doesn't apply it as thick. In fact, she reminds me of Before. The light touch. The fine line.

"Yes."

"Okay ..."

"You've always needed taking care of," Annie says. "Besides, there are times I can't sleep." She shrugs. "I peek around the house. Look in on you. Check on Mom and Dad."

Annie turns. Stares at her image in the mirror. "Did you know," she says, using a voice that could be in a documentary, "that fat people have fewer wrinkles?"

It's been a long time since we've been in here getting ready at the same time. I hadn't realized until now that I missed this.

"Huh?"

"It's true. Look at us both." She pulls me to her side. Clutches at my elbow. Makes me look at us. The Twins Who Are So Different. "No wrinkles. For either of us actually."

"Wrinkles?" I ask. "We turned sixteen a month ago."

"I know."

"That makes no sense," I say. "Neither of us ..." Then I'm laughing. Hard. Crumpled over. There's still a bit of toothpaste on my mouth. Annie looks at me. She raises her eyebrows. Then she lets out this laugh I haven't heard in forever, a belly laugh. Huge. Loud.

Man, it feels good to laugh with her like this. I've missed my sister.

I rinse my hands, bits of giggles splashing down the drain with the warm water. Annie comes closer. Flattens my hair with her palms. "You have the best hair," she says. And pat pat pats at me.

"I used to want your hair." I stop. "I didn't mean that."

She shakes her hair at me. "Don't want it anymore?"

I feel my eyes widen.

"It's okay. Chopping off one's own hair can have ugly results."

Then she says, "Sarah? Do you think I'm sexy?"

She's serious, though there's laughter leftover in her voice. Will she dance around singing in her off-key voice that old, old song Mom used to listen to when we were little? But Annie asks again, "Do you?"

"What do you mean?" I wipe my hands free of water and leftover conditioner.

I know what she means because I look at myself that way. To see if I've changed since Garret dumped me, to see if there was a reason for him to listen to his mom. To see if I ever have a chance with anyone else.

Alex maybe?

Annie's hands are on her hips. Her feet spread. She dabs at her eyes so she doesn't mess up her makeup. She's snapped her bra and pulled on an Elton John shirt. Now she tugs on her blue jeans, and before they're fastened she uses a sultry voice. "To a man. Do you think I'm appealing?"

I see in her eyes she really wants to know.

My cheeks flush. I think of Garret and then, for some reason, Alex. "A-peeling?" I say, hoping to end this conversation. "That sounds like something you do to fruit. And anyway, you can't think sexy about a relative, Annie. Ick."

My sister is so comfortable with herself. She's had so many boyfriends. Was so popular. Best friend to so many girls, so many people.

She laughed about her period, talked openly about staying a virgin, didn't care what people thought when she wore her crown and strutted to high school in heels.

Now I squeeze the face towel I've dried off with. It took me two weeks to hold Garret's hand in public. Three weeks before I let him kiss me. *You are not the same as your sister*, comes into my head. *Garret doesn't care. Alex won't.*

Annie's insistent. The sexy voice gone. "Do you think men would find me attractive now?"

I sling the towel over the side of the tub. "Men? Men shouldn't be looking at you," I say. Though I know they do. Did. Do? Is it still do?

She nods, says, "Yes. Men. My face is almost the same, don't you think, Sarah?" She's quiet a second. There's that hesitation that's so not Annie. That's more me. "Or do you agree with Mom?"

"Like I told you, Annie," I say, "I think you're beautiful."

"Do you think I might catch something from these other people? The club people?"

"Mom didn't say that." My words are breathy.

Annie glances at herself. "She meant it."

"The club is a good thing." Annie's voice, soft like her body, floats around me. "Thanks for caring, Sis."

"Always," I say.

annie

When Sarah leaves
I look at myself.
No means no.
Even if, at first, you thought you meant yes.
Even if, at first, it was your fault.
Even if, at first, you made yourself available.

sarah

I'm thinking about a test in Chemistry when Annie says, "He's out there again."

The morning is clear and dark. No clouds. To the east, a thin line of morning shows, skimming the earth like icing.

"Who?" Will the car never warm up?

"Floyd Freeman."

I stare out my window. Yup, there he is, shoveling. And his driveway is clear. My stomach does this weird falling thing. "Maybe he's crazy."

"For a while, every time I saw him, I wanted to run," Annie says. "And Sarah, it's Mom who's crazy. All that crap last night."

"What do you mean, run?" I asked, but Annie interrupts.

"She hurt my feelings. Again. Telling me I look bad."

"I know."

Maybe it's worse watching what has happened to me all these years happen to Annie now. I'm used to it. I was trained that way. But this is new-ish to her.

Half a block from school, we pull into the line of cars waiting to turn into the parking lot. The sides of the road are piled with dirty snow. A few trees have limbs snapped by the weather and now hang like broken arms. Mailboxes look like expensive cupcakes with too much whipped cream on top. Annie swears under her breath. I'm not sure if this is because the hill we coast down is dangerously icy or if she's still mad at Mr. Freeman or if she's frustrated with high school traffic.

Annie clutches at the steering wheel and I'm glad, again, I don't drive.

"Don't give her the power," I say. "You don't have to wear the black dress. Choose something else."

Annie might not hear me because she doesn't answer.

When we pull into a spot, people are piling out of their cars. A handful of kids hurry to the seminary building to study religion for an hour. Others run into the main building. Leafless trees clatter bony limbs as the wind blows snow into drifts.

Chemistry is in my head. Chemistry. Why did I take Chemistry? I knew it wouldn't be easy.

Annie turns off the car. She sits there, quiet, and I don't move. I'm not sure why I'm not out of here and headed to class as fast as I can walk so I can get some last-minute studying done.

"Once I packed up all my stuff in the car," Annie says. "To go. Loaded the trunk because I knew no one would check it."

A car alarm goes off. People call to one another.

"Why?"

She takes a deep breath, which is funny because I can't breathe at all. "Have you ever thought of running off for good? You know, never coming back?"

A snowball hits the car and I jump. Someone laughs. The tree we're parked under reaches toward the hood.

I shake my head no.

My skin is plastic.

"Oh," Annie says. Then she opens the door, slams it behind her, and heads off to class.

sarah

L eaving me alone after saying something like that. The brat.

sarah

The first bell rings. Then the second. I'm going to flunk Chemistry if I keep going late. That's what I think, but I don't move. I wonder about Floyd Freeman shoveling non-existent snow. Or shoveling in a storm. Wonder about Annie. What's going on between the two of them?

What's made my pacifist sister so mad? Should I talk to Mom? There's no way Annie'd forgive me for going behind her back. What's wrong?

The worry is like weights. We were just laughing about wrinkles, about being sexy. And now she says this? Right after she sees Mr. Freeman?

I sit in the car until I'm so cold I can't stay any longer. The lot is cleared of people. Cars are parked skewampus. A cloud moves in from the north. Low. Almost touching the ground, it seems. Another storm. This one with lightning, something that doesn't happen often. Already, thunder rolls closer.

I can't go to class. Can't walk in late where everyone will see me. The thought makes my mouth go dry.

So I wait in the bathroom until second period starts. Those dark clouds have now covered the school. It's like we're in some fantasy story, the way things look outside.

What's Mr. Freeman doing now? Does he stand in his drive-way, watch the storm come in, and maybe look toward our home the way Annie looks at him as we drive past his place? The hair on my arms raises at the possibility.

sarah

Why is there so much to worry about? I'm hardly sixteen and there's trouble with my parents. Trouble with my sister. Trouble with my anxieties. I want things to be the way they were Before. Way before. Like when I was little, begging my mother for cookies, and she lifted me up on her hip, letting me point to one still hot on the pan.

I'm not stupid. I know there are all kinds of crap out there. And Annie's got me thinking. Believing Tommy Jones and Mr. Freeman are both guilty.

Where does it start? Did someone who is a rapist today try to have his way with girls when he was in high school, like Tommy Jones? Did he hold them in the halls and force himself on them?

Did someone who's now a murderer bully kids in class? Did he write horrible notes?

Are we born this way? Born to hurt? To kill? To love? To serve?

What about home? Is what's going on at home because of a workload? Frazzled nerves? Someone trying to keep up with the Joneses?

Or only about parents watching a child grow heavier and heavier when they can do nothing about it.

Is being ignored abuse? If your mother doesn't see you and

your father only notices that you aren't like your sister, what is that? Are Mom and Dad responsible at all?

And why all this with Annie? I've been wondering about that for months.

sarah

At my locker, the hall like Grand Central Station, I dig for books. I'm jostled, shoved once, and witness a couple making out right next to me.

Ick.

Get a room, I want to say. But I don't have the courage. Annie would holler that, laugh afterward.

Something in Annie's locker catches my eye. A bit of folded paper stuffed in an air vent. Not again.

Does this happen to her every day?

"Homer," someone yells. "Debate team meeting right now."

"Coming," someone else answers.

Cold air swirls around my feet. A door to outside was opened down the way. It feels good with all these bodies hurrying to classes. With people breathing my air. And kissing in my personal space.

"Dang it." I pull at the paper, heart hammering, but can't get it out. Whoever stuffed it in here wedged it in tight. That last note—I won't think the words—is in my head. I have to get rid of this new one, so I open Annie's locker myself.

There are lots of notes in here and several tumble to the floor.

Who?

Why?

I scoop them up, but they fall again. So I push the paper into a pile. Some are wet from damp shoes and dirty puddles of water.

"Did you see who did this, who left these?" I ask the couple.

"Notes," the girl says, standing on tiptoe. "Cool."

"Did you see?"

She shakes her head. "You're the first person here since me and Abe stopped."

"Thanks," I say. For what? Talking to strangers has given me a pounding headache.

The kissers leave, arm in arm, saying how much they love each other.

Each piece of paper — and there are at least twenty of them — says something grotesque. Like *stop eating* and *pig* and *ugly*. Stupid stuff. Cruel stuff. I stand there, because I can't believe this. Then, fast as I can, I shovel the paper out, crumple it, stuff it into my backpack.

Home school is best for you. Keep you away from us.

And the worst one, *Just di-et.*

They want her to die?

Slut. Whore.

The writing's the same. All blocky. One person wrote all of this. Tommy.

My mouth feels raw. I can't quite see because of the headache, and I'm sick to my stomach. The halls clear, and I'm late again. I'm spending more time this week in the hall than in the classroom.

I don't get it. Annie is far from the heaviest person in school. She's not that overweight. Yes, she's gained weight, but I can think of lots of fat kids. And teachers.

Do they get picked on too?

I search Annie's locker. Look for everything. Look until I am

159

sure the evidence is gone. Take it all. I'll throw it away. Burn it. Something. She packed up to leave.

"Hey."

I let out a little yelp, then turn to see Melanie. I don't realize until I'm looking at her that I've been crying.

I close Annie's locker. "What are you doing here?" I have this urge to slap Melanie. For ignoring Annie. For no longer being her friend. And maybe, maybe—"Did you do this to Annie?"

It's all I can do to speak up.

Melanie comes closer. "What are you talking about?"

I swallow. "The notes," I say. Wipe at my eyes.

"What notes?"

My fingers feel like ice. "They were in her locker."

Melanie picks up a slip of paper from the floor. Something I missed. She reads it, then tightens a fist around it. "No," she says between clenched teeth. "I didn't. I was checking to see where Annie is. She skipped class again."

Again. And then ... Oh no.

"She found them," I say.

sarah

We look for her in bathrooms, in the class she's supposed to be in with Melanie, check with the nurse. Two teachers tell us to get to class, but neither of us answers. Melanie does a good job staying up with me even though she wears spiked heels and a short skirt that flounces with each step.

Peering out at the parking lot, I see our car's gone.

"I need to go home," I say. We live only a few miles from school. I can walk.

"Let me take you," Melanie says.

I hesitate then say, "Yes. Thank you. Okay."

It's a quiet drive, like the search was. Neither of us speaks. The sun shines, making the snow a mirror for the light. My eyes water again, but I can't cry now.

When she pulls into my driveway, Melanie puts the car in park, and before I can open the door she says, "Look, Sarah." She lets out a sigh. "I know you've blamed me for ending my friendship with Annie, but I didn't quit being her friend."

The door is cracked open, and cold air edges in. The heated driveway is wet, but clear. That's what Mr. Freeman needs. A heated driveway.

"What are you talking about?"

"Annie is one of my best friends." She waits. "She was one of my best friends." Melanie stops talking again. "I still want to be her best friend. I've called, texted. Even cornered her at school. But she's quit doing stuff with me."

I stare at Melanie. "That's not true."

She nods. "It is. Annie hasn't done anything with anybody from our group, Sarah. You know that."

I don't answer.

"I wouldn't hurt her feelings. I love her. This whole thing has been hard on me too. I want my friend back."

I sit there a second longer. Then I open the door the rest of the way and get out of the car. The wind blows, hard, kicking iced snow up. It glitters in the air.

"I miss her," she says again.

I raise my hand in a weak goodbye. "Thanks," I say. "Thanks for helping me."

"Of course," she says.

annie

School is
   *bodies doors toomanysounds touching groping
swearing laughing screaming calling talking dancing
bells smells crowds whistles catcalls whining kissing
grabbing slapping crying wishing panic hating loving
eating commands orders cropping fighting lectures.*
   And notes.
   Too many notes.

annie

The curtains are closed
but I peek out
when I hear the car.
Melanie and Sarah?
Together?
She's brought my sister
home.

Melanie used to
tease Sarah
because she
seems to
blend in
with the world.
Sarah doesn't stand out
flounce
swirl.
But follows the edges of halls
and sits at the sides of classrooms.
Away.
Alone.

It's like she isn't quite here.
Some people pick up on that.
Some people see it.
Go in for the kill.
Melanie is with Sarah now.
Saying what?
Being kind?
I stand here
my heart weepy.

I had planned to go back
get her myself.
Be waiting in
the car.
Not desert her.
Not leave her stranded.

I peek out
the window, cheesecake
on a plate in my hand.

Tears slip down my cheeks as
I watch my sister
my best friend.

Are they the same person now?

annie

I feel guilty about that past.

annie

You made me, it's your
fault
I love you
You were so beautiful

No one can care like I do
like I do
No one will love you this way
this way

This is all the same
in
my
head

annie

Some nights
it's too dark for words
and I lie in bed
the blankets like weights
the sound of the heater
like a train
anxiety
forcing me out of bed
to the bathroom
where I get in the tub
fully clothed
and try to calm my breathing
calm my heart

ease
the memories

erase
the past

sarah

Annie?"

She sits in the front room, a black blotch on the white furniture. Elton John peers out from her shirt, his huge glasses what I notice first.

"Melanie brought me home."

Annie doesn't move.

Mom's running the vacuum around upstairs.

"Who did it?"

Nothing.

"Annie," I say.

There have to be words. The right words. The words that support. I'm the girl who punched someone in the nose for calling Annie ugly. Sure, we were five. But it's proof fear doesn't need to control me.

"It's Jones, isn't it?"

Annie looks up at me. She seems so small, sitting there in this princess chair. "What difference does it make? They've suspended him once. What good will this do, you knowing?"

"Just tell me."

Annie hesitates. Then nods. "I've seen him do it," she says.

I kiss Annie on the cheek. "I love you."

Then I leave the formal living room. Get my set of keys and go out to the car that I've driven only a handful of times.

I'm going back to school. Shaking. Scared. Crazy, maybe. But Tommy Jones needs to be knocked off his bike and right on his butt.

sarah

With no traffic it doesn't take long to get to the high school. There wasn't even one near miss. Pulling into visitor parking, sweat on my upper lip, I think perhaps I could drive again if needed.

"Hope I'm never needed," I say.

The air stings, it's so cold. The notes are shoved in my pants pockets and in my jacket as well. Melanie threw a handful away.

Here's the deal. It's not like the movies.

I don't storm into Ms. Cleland's office and sling notes onto her desk. I don't swear and holler and follow Tommy to his classroom and kick him in his ... manhood. Or lack thereof. ·

It takes forty minutes of waiting to see the vice principal. And when I show her the notes, I keep my voice calm and try not to pass out.

"We'll take care of this," Ms. Cleland says. She's angry, I can see that. "This is distasteful, to say the least. And bullying of any sort is not allowed here."

"What will happen?"

"Suspension to start," she says. "There is the past incident that we have to take into consideration." She pauses. "And I need Annie to come in and talk to me. I need to know how long this has been going on. If there has been a new … assault. Or anything else."

The chair I sit in is uncomfortable. Is that by design or is it how I feel? "She might not," I say. "She hasn't told you about the other notes."

Ms. Cleland nods. "I'll talk to her. And maybe you could encourage her to come and see me?" She stands. "Head on back to class now."

I stand too. Nod. Lie by saying nothing.

"Sarah?"

I turn back to Ms. Cleland. "Yes, ma'am?"

"Thanks for coming in here when Annie wouldn't."

I swallow. "Sure."

When I get back to where I parked, I throw up in a pile of snow, expecting the bees I feel I've swallowed to buzz away like something from a Stephen King movie. My stomach's empty when I get in the car, and now I have the dry heaves. This is going to be a long drive home.

annie

Some secrets must be kept.
No
matter
the
consequences.

sarah

Annie's on the phone when I walk back into the living room. Talking to who? Ms. Cleland? Tears run down her face. Her voice is low. I leave Annie alone. She needs time. I know I would. She sort of nods at me when I pass.

Maybe things will change now. For all of us.

Just like that, I'm overcome with fatigue. I'm not sure I'll make it up the stairs, past the hallway pictures. I'm not sure I can open my door, can even turn the knob. But I do.

I fall on my bed. A sigh escapes.

I love my room.

Love that I feel safe here. Something I've not fully realized until right now. Calm. Like me with no pressure. I can breathe. If I had the energy, I'd get up and lock the door.

annie

I know from my own life   secrets can be
                              deadly.
Enough secrets and
you weave a
pattern
that ends up all lies.

they have for me.

I thought I could
control it all and now I see
this controls
me.

sarah

I dream of a stranger who talks in muffled tones. Annie answers. Ms. Cleland is in her office and she whispers to me through the door. Tells me to mind my own business but still watch out for Annie.

"How can I do both?" I ask.

I'm in the hall. My feet are heavy, tired, it seems, and no matter how I tug to free myself, I can't.

I can't get to Annie, who's crying now.

I just can't move.

thursday

sarah

The next morning, when I wander into the kitchen, Dad says over coffee, "Party Saturday night. You know the procedure." Then he leaves. Doesn't even say goodbye. Didn't speak to Mom. Have they stopped talking altogether? Is work that important?

My throat squeezes. Will they get divorced?

Mom's awake and close to Annie, who sips hot chocolate. From here I can see the marshmallows floating in the cup. She looks at me over the top of the mug.

I pretend Dad didn't leave.

"Are you okay?" I keep my voice low in case Mom doesn't know what happened.

"I told her," Annie says. "About everything. We're talking to Dad after the party."

"Annie's choice," Mom says, and her eyes fill with tears.

"No more crying," Annie says. "It's all right. Sarah took care of it yesterday."

I sit at the table, in my place, next to my sister and across from the French doors. The days are getting longer. There's a world outside the glass, not just a hint of the sun. And my mother is freaking out over me.

And being nice.

"Sarah," Mom says at long last, and the tears spill. "Thank you for defending your sister."

"Breakfast?" Annie asks and she's up to make me something. Hot chocolate to start. She pours the drink from the pan. I bet she used a chocolate bar, half and half, real vanilla bean, and sugar.

"Sure, Mom," I say.

"I know it was hard for you. I know I've been hard on you."

I'm not sure what to say.

Annie gives me the hot chocolate, then she hugs me, tight. Her sweater, the color of new roses, is soft on my face. In the glass of the doors, we're ghosts. But we're both smiling.

"You gonna survive Dad's event?" she asks.

My smile dissolves. I don't want to think of it. These get-togethers are hell to me. Hell decorated to the hilt, with the splashes of lights and colors and people. So many people. The performance, whether I want it or not.

"Sure," I say. "I'll be fine."

Mom and Annie are dressed already. I need to get moving. I think that, but I'm still, frozen by the thought of a stupid party. If I can talk to Ms. Cleland, can't I wander in my own house filled with strangers for a few hours?

We've had parties with so many people that strangers have walked in thinking we wouldn't notice. This one won't be as large. There's the merger to consider.

I sip the hot chocolate, grateful Annie and I are doing a piece we've played before. One I know by heart so I can close my eyes and not think of anyone watching me.

"You all right?" she asks.

I nod.

If I don't think about it, I'll be okay.

annie

I watch Sarah.
Feel the guilt
in my veins.
I knew she was shy
knew she hated this public life
but never cared
because I was a professional
entertainer.

So I make breakfast for her,
like that will help.
Pour milk over steamy
oatmeal
add sugar
and fresh berries.

Mom is consumed with a list,
pushing back her hair with one hand,
writing with the other.
She doesn't see
my sister.
Not now that she's thinking of the

party of the year
and the problem with Tommy Jones
is over
as far as she is concerned.

Sarah sits at the table
taking slow,
deep breaths.

What was it like for her yesterday?
To approach the vice principal?

Something pinches at my heart.
How did I let Sarah
get to this place
and stay there
alone

when she was so willing to help me?

sarah

Instead of enjoying the breakfast Annie makes, I worry about Dad's party. Blush at the idea of standing in front of everyone. All those eyes. People holding drinks. Wandering in from wherever they've been at the house. Coming to stand where Annie and I will be. Me, in front of the piano with my violin, the way I have to be. Annie announcing the piece.

"Don't borrow trouble," Mom has told me. And she means, don't think about it. Don't fret.

But I know me.

Even if I don't think of Saturday night, it will be there. At the edges of my mind. When I take the sign language test. The Chemistry make up. When I walk to class. When I'm sad about Garret. Angry about Tommy. Wondering about Annie. It will be there, in the periphery. Waiting for me.

annie

The truth is I helped.
I swallow at my guilt.
I helped Sarah
feel crappy
when I let Melanie tease her
when I saw she was afraid and laughed
when I knew someone tormented her in middle school
and said nothing.
"Here you go.
Made with love," I say
handing over the oatmeal,
and my voice
cracks.

annie

No emotions will show
at the party
and
I'll keep Sarah
by my side.

Keep us both safe.

sarah

When we were little—before the fear, before the crowns, before the comparisons, before the failures, before Before—Annie and I were the same person.

I remember that as she pushes the oatmeal over to me. Like she used to do when we were younger. "Thank you," I say. Maybe I can perform with her. I've done big things lately. Maybe, if Annie and I are headed where we used to be Before, I can do it.

Are we becoming the same again?

At school I keep my mind where it should be. On studies. In the classroom, I try not to think if Tommy will be in Sign. I don't look ahead at what waits on Saturday. I don't look behind at a boy who didn't choose me in the end.

In design class, I glance out the window, where winter tries to invade the room. Alex asks me to help him come up with a limerick about the football team, and we laugh at everything that rhymes with jock. At one point he says, "Maybe we can get dinner some time," and I say, "That would be fun," and my heart clenches because I'm doing what my sister said. I'm moving on.

But when the thought comes of a house full of people, of men and women drinking, and laughing, growing louder, more insistent, telling jokes, demanding I pull out my violin, I feel myself fold up, get smaller, and there's a moment I hope I can breathe.

This weather strangles me sometimes too, when there's no place to escape. No house to run to. No place to hike or walk or run away.

And yet in the morning, before anyone has awakened, I can peer out the back window, over the darkened fields, and the world seems so huge and empty. A place someone could get lost in. Nothing but snow and stars and air so cold you'd freeze and not even care.

sarah

Outside of Chemistry (I'm sure I passed the make-up exam), Garret stands waiting. He has on a black sweatshirt and his hair looks so blond. Should it be fair that he has such blond hair in the winter?

"Garret," I say. I don't even mean to. His name falls out of my mouth and he smiles. Gosh, he has the best smile. Those white teeth.

"Hi, Sarah."

I've stopped in the classroom doorway and people shove past. Alex comes up behind Garret and raises his eyebrows at me.

"Hey," Alex says. He's smiling as well.

"Hi."

"Move," someone says, pushing me, and I say, "Sorry."

Oh. Oh. This is … Why am I embarrassed? As though I've done something wrong.

Lockers slam. I can hear a teacher hollering about no home-work for the weekend and yes, you're welcome, thank you very much. Annie walks toward me and someone screams down the hall. The intercom comes on with a crackle.

Close behind my sister is her old best friend.

annie

Melanie is …
I won't list adjectives that fill my brain
want to leap from my tongue.

Sarah leaves,
sliding a little on a wet part of the floor. I'm stabbed to
the center.

I pass a classroom window
and for a moment
see myself as I was —

Yes, the hair has changed
and the make
up
but
the window is a trick mirror
and I am thin again.

I look
See myself
Before.

A sudden, desperate feeling goes through me.
I want to be that
girl again.
I want to be thin.

I
was
like Melanie.

I
was Melanie.

But I can make me new.
Not take back all the old.
Be there for my sister.
Right?

sarah

You worried about the party?" Annie asks. She's found me in ASL class. Miss Saunders stands at the front of the room, saying hello as we walk in, waiting for the bell to ring.

"Can't talk about it without wanting to puke," I say. Throwing up once in the school parking lot is enough for me.

Corny as it is, I'm grinning because my sister came to see me. She knew I needed her. "What?" Annie asks, and she smiles too.

"You're going to be late," I say, but I link my arm through hers.

"Sisters?" Miss Saunders signs.

I nod. "Twins," I sign back.

"I see that. Same nose. Same smile. Both pretty."

Miss Saunders turns her attention to other people entering the classroom. There will be no Tommy today. Because of me.

No. Because of me.

Nervousness crawls through me.

We have three minutes to whisper before the first bell rings. For a class where no one is to use their voice, it's pretty loud in here. If your teacher can't hear you, well, you can get away with a lot.

Annie looks around the room. I feel her flinch. She turns to me. "Stay away from the guys in this class," she says.

"Who else?" I ask. Who?

But Miss Saunders is saying it's time to begin. "Go!" she says in sign language. "Tell your sister she needs to vamoose."

Annie understands. She doesn't even wait for me to translate. Just leaves.

annie

I didn't know Jared Parker
and
Ben Adams were in this class.
Yes, I knew about Tommy.

But the jerks who held me
that day
stopped me, allowed Tommy Jones to rub
up against me and
put his filthy mouth on mine?

They're here.

Jared sees me. Looks surprised.
Glances away.
He stumbles getting to his chair.

He apologized after
The Incident.
Called me. Said he wasn't thinking,
said he would never
never

do anything like that to anyone again.
That he would never
never
treat a girl
like that again.

But Ben. Looking at him now
I can see he's mad — that Tommy's gone?
Why else?

A
smile
crawls onto his face
filled with anger.

Did he write the notes too?
Even with a promise of expulsion?
Who knows.
Who cares.
I turn my back to him
whisper to my sister
and
go.

annie

encounters with Tommy
those first few times.
Ben and Jared with him.
laughing as
he stopped me in the hall

(before the weight)

grabbed my arm
asked
for services someone had rumored I gave.

As I walk from the ASL class
room
back
straight
this deaf teacher
looks me in the eyes
sees my soul
then glances at Sarah
and motions for me to
Go!
Go!
Go!

annie

I'm so humiliated.

annie

still

sarah

I see the change in her face. Miss Saunders is talking, talking, and I run after Annie. Someone tips too far in a chair and almost falls. People laugh.

"Hey, Sarah," Miss Saunders signs to me, stepping to the door. Watching me.

My sister. That's all I sign.

Miss Saunders nods once.

Annie's moving fast. I have to jog to keep up.

"What happened? Annie?"

"I'm leaving," she says. The hall is cleared out. Her backpack hangs from her arm. Slaps at her leg. Weak light falls through the skylights. So weak it can't even splash on the floor.

I stop, watch her walk away. Hesitate. And then …

"Wait," I say, before she goes through the door to snowflakes that look like they might change their minds and go back heaven-ward. "I'm coming with you."

Back into my classroom. A quick apology to the teacher. Grab my books. And run to Annie, who doesn't even check out of school.

These last few days …

They've felt like an eternity.

They've gone on forever.

They have weighed more than the whole school year before as the story has unfolded and I've seen more about my sister.

We're finding each other. That's almost as scary as the other stuff. Because what if I fail her somehow? Or fail me?

"I'm coming." A thought crowds my brain, pushing at me. *Is Tommy Jones the reason Annie must protect herself with weight?*

"Where to?" Annie says when I run up to her. She stands on the sidewalk and I'm worried we're gonna get called back inside, get a call from the truant officer.

A few flakes of snow fall. Slowing down. Maybe it's too cold for them too.

"You decide," I say. And we're off to the car, my heart pounding, and Annie's telling me about Jared and Ben. The apology. The hate.

"Oh," I say, again and again.

We drive around town until Annie stops shaking. Till she can tell how she felt that day in an empty hallway. How she felt when Jared apologized. How she's known that Ben is still bent out of shape because her actions messed with his college possibilities.

"But the notes." I'm picking at my nails. Have pulled one off too low. "It shows he doesn't care."

"Right," she says.

We drive on. Pass Dad's office.

"I hate that place," my sister says.

Pass the high school twice, like a dare.

"I hate that place too."

Pass the community center where Annie participated in a few pageants when she was younger. This is the venue that asked her to be a guest judge. "That place," she says, her voice as slow motion as those few snowflakes. "That place I don't mind."

After a bit Annie says, "Sarah. Maybe I'm starting a diet. You know. A diet of healthy eating."

"What?" I sit up straight in my seat. Nurse my finger.

"Sure. I think I've decided to. Don't tell Mom. I don't want her crawling all over me."

The car is warm and I think this Tommy Jones thing is over. It's over. I laugh. Happy to be in on the secret. "Are you serious? Why? I thought you wanted …" I pause.

"I know. To be this way." Annie's quiet. "It's time to do the hard things and face what's happened. And why not?" Annie says. She doesn't look me in the eye.

"Of course. Why not?"

And then, "I am so glad, Annie. Glad this is what you want."

She changes lanes without signaling. "Let's get doughnuts as a sendoff. My treat."

The road is full of traffic. The whole town looks dirty because of the old snow, the lifeless looking trees, the sky like an upside-down pot of scrubbed steel.

So this is what Springfield looks like when we're in school. I never really thought about how life goes on when I'm not there. How Dad goes into the office. How Mom stays at home.

We park the car and go into the Krispy Kreme store that smells so yeasty and sweet my mouth waters. Order tea and three doughnuts (each!) and eat one standing at the counter.

"Now where?" Annie says. "We're killing time. We don't have to do anything unless we want to."

"I know." I lick glaze from my fingers. Peek in the bag at the remaining doughnuts. Hesitate before I speak. "It's like Before. Or before Before. You know, when we were friends."

Annie hugs me. Not a one-armed hug, but a tight, close-to-her embrace. "I don't know how it happened," she says, "but I've missed this, this being with you."

"Me too."

My sister kisses my face, pushes my hair back. "Let's get out of here."

I grab her hand and we slip and slide outside, all the way to the car.

annie

Here's what I think. What I know.
Popular people feel
>   *lonely heartbroken sad stressed used tired*
>   *angry bullied frustrated annoyed isolated broken-*
>   *hearted abused anxious overworked*
the same as anyone else.
We aren't allowed to show pain.
If you complain
you're made fun of.
If you say you're too tired
too bored
too far behind
someone will say "Suck it up."

annie

Making a change now
could be
dangerous.
Could be bad
for my health.
Losing weight.
fewer doughnuts
less candy
no nighttime snacks
empty drawers

I think of that thin girl
in the reflection
at school,
the thin me.
Then I think of Tommy
and
others
the
Other
and I'm scared. Scared.

Today
I don't want to be with anyone
except Sarah.

annie

*"Tell me how this all
started with Tommy," she says.*

Tell me.

sarah

We're sipping tea. Eating the last of our doughnuts. Annie speaks. The kind of monologue where I can tell she's not saying everything.

First it's, "We're not going to Dad's dumb party."

She sounds eight years old and I laugh, relief flooding through me. No violin! No duet! No people to push through, be introduced to, to try to talk to.

"If you don't," I say, "I won't either." I sit back in the seat. Close my eyes. Taste sugar on my lips.

Wait.

"Guys," Annie says. "They're so dumb. Even Garret."

Even Alex? I almost want to ask Annie what she thinks but this is her time. Her story. And for once I don't mind hiding my own from view.

"Yes, Sarah," Annie says. Her eyes are so green in this gray world. She's finished that second doughnut. She swirls her tea around in the cup. There's a dark red lipstick print on the lid. "Garret was a fool. Is a fool. He doesn't deserve you. To dump you because his mom said so. You two had a great thing."

My heart has moved into my throat.

"I'm sorry it happened."

An older lady pulls up next to us in the parking lot. She has on a cream-colored coat (is cream even a color?) and she seems like the only bright bit out there today. She walks into Dillard's.

I'm so grateful to hear Annie say this about Garret. How I didn't do anything wrong, I don't know whether to bawl or laugh.

"Jared had a crush on me." Annie looks out the window like she's driving. Hands on the steering wheel and everything. "The guy from your sign language class?"

"Okay."

"And Ben was always there. Whenever Jared talked to me, there was Ben. It was strange."

It's snowing now. Icy sleet, really. A truck sails out of the parking lot and to the red light, almost rolling into traffic.

"Guys," Annie says. "They can be real jerks. Young and old. All of them."

And our talk is done.

annie

They were Dumb and
Dumber
Bumbling around
And I shouted no
shouted at Jared to leave me alone

And he did.

sarah

Girls," Dad says late that night. He slaps his hands together, rubs them like he can create a fire. "We're expecting a crowd."

"No children this time," Mom says. She looks beautiful today. Relieved. Like the Tommy knowledge has freed her. "Thank goodness. No one ever watches their kids."

I look up from my laptop at Annie. Mom is exhilarated. At her best. She's had the cleaning ladies over, ordered all the food and wine.

Dad folds the *New York Times*, picks up his phone that's beeped at him. It runs his life, that phone.

"And you too, Sarah," Dad says. "No more of this shy stuff. I need you to push through and be your best self. This is important to me. Executives are coming in from Florida. We all need to shine. Okay?"

"Dad," I say. There's a fist where my heart used to be.

"Didn't I tell you?" Annie says, "We're not going to be here." She's in her jammies. Showered already. No one knows, but she was in the basement on the treadmill.

"I'm out of shape, Sarah," she'd said earlier when I let myself in to chat with her. She grinned when she spoke, sweat dripping off her face.

Now our father looks at both of us. For a moment I envision him before success, before shy and overweight daughters. In my memory he looks like he used to. Like he did when we were more important than money. Gosh, he used to laugh with us. I'd forgotten that.

He says, "You'll be here." He glances at me. Eyes Annie. "Both of you." He's pointing. Emphasizing the words. "This is a family affair."

Dad doesn't wait for an answer. Just leaves. Where's he going this late? I hear the door to the garage open then close.

Annie and I look at Mom. That fist is pounding in my chest. Pounding at my ribs. This is all too much for me.

"Sometimes …," Mom says and then she stops herself. The tired mom I'm used to shows up again.

Then Dad is back. Standing in the doorway of the front room.

"Daddy," I say. I don't mean to sound scared.

"Annie. Sarah," Dad says.

We all stare at him. "Look. I'm sorry. I've lost myself."

He steps closer then backs up.

"This crap you've been dealing with at school, Annie. Your mother told me about it last night and I should have been there for it. For you." He stops talking. "I should have known. Stopped it."

I glance at Annie, who stands there with her mouth hanging open.

"But I've let work get in the way. I'm so sorry."

He opens his hands to us, palms out. I'm too surprised to answer.

"You don't have to do it. You don't have to do anything. But if you'll forgive me, both of you, for not being here for the last little while …"

Mom makes this sad sound in her throat.

It's our old father standing there. The one who used to spend time with us. Took off work and insisted we stay home from school so we could do things with him.

A hush goes over the room. Annie looks at me. I nod at her.

"Daddy," Annie says, "you're forgiven. And of course we'll play for you and Mom. It's our tradition."

She runs to him. Throws her arms around his neck. He rests his head on hers.

"I'll try," I say. "I'll try." I'm welcomed into the hug.

annie

He expected more,
Wanted more,
Asked for more,
And I gave it.

annie

Hands
grab
pull
want
ask
demand.

"If you loved me. If you loved me."
I wake, a scream tearing out of me.

In the dark I can see a slice of my face in the mirror.

I don't want to be alone.
Not anymore.

The club.
My parents?
For sure, my sister.

Can I make these choices?

sarah

That night, after the doughnuts and time with Annie, the hugs from Dad and then Mom, all of us together, I dream of snow. Too much. Fast-falling. Blinding. It fills my mouth. I'm freezing to death.

Annie pokes me awake. At first I'm not sure if this is part of my dreaming. I squint at her.

"What?" I'm trembling from cold.

"Let me in bed with you," Annie says.

Her voice is low and I wonder if steam comes from her lips or if that's my imagination still in this room.

"Okay." I slide over, and Annie gets into bed.

She's a heater. She warms my cold feet, cold hands, snuggles against my back.

I'm almost asleep, positioned the way we used to scrooch up to each other. In fact, I'm dreaming of snow again. And a black tree that grows tiny buds of leaves.

Annie whispers, "Sarah, I'm afraid."

I jerk awake.

"What?" I ask.

But there's no answer.

friday

sarah

When we get into the car (warmed already!), I'm surprised at a handwritten note.

"Look at this," I say. "It's a thank you. From Dad."

Annie stares at me, the car idling. She tilts her head a little, like she can't believe what I've just said. "What?" She grabs the paper from my hand. Reads the words I've seen, "Thank you, girls. I love you both," then stares at me again.

"What is going on with them?" Annie says. She's whispering. Reverent. "Did you notice Mom was civil? More than civil?"

I nod.

There is something strange about what's happening in our family. This change in Dad just as Annie decides to lose weight and I decide to no longer think of Garret. All of us shifting at once. Is it in the air?

"Sometimes," Annie says, still looking at me, the card in her fingers. I can barely hear her over the heater. "Sometimes I think everything will be okay if …" She pauses, "… If they would just be okay with who we are."

I nod. Yes. I know that feeling. That please-let-me-be-who-I-am-and-love-me-still feeling.

We're backing out of the garage. She's handed me the card

and I hold it against my chest. It's like warm weather has filled the car.

"He was human last night."

Last night.

Annie coming into my room. That dream. This card from Dad. All strange.

We head off down the road. The sun is bright, the sky clear. The snow reflects the light and is blinding.

"I'm glad," I say. "We've all been so ..." I can't think of the word.

"Off?" Annie says.

"Broken."

"Yes," Annie says. "That's it."

I tuck the message from Dad into my backpack.

Mr. Freeman stands in the driveway, looking in the direction of the sun.

"Why doesn't he go inside?" Annie says.

"He's so old."

I glance at Annie as we drive past Mr. Freeman, who doesn't look in our direction. Something about him makes me feel sad. His loneliness maybe? My loneliness?

"Does he have dementia?" I ask.

"Who cares?" Annie says. Then we're racing to school again.

annie

Today, after classes, we'll meet.
There are nine people so far.
Kids I've spoken to about this
who might need it.
Nine without any real advertising.
How's that?

I know for a fact everyone at school could come here.
But they won't.
They're too good to admit
we're all the same.

They are like I used to be.

annie

*I peek in at Sarah
during Sign class,
watch my sister.*

I can see she's a natural.

*She looks
happy.
Unafraid.
Like she did yesterday
when we were in the car
together.*

*There's a difference in her face.
A calm.*

*A thought floors me.
What it would be like to be afraid
every
minute?*

Not only at night?

sarah

I get a text from Dad, asking me to work for him that afternoon. He even comes to school to pick me up after classes are over.

"I need you to do some last-minute filing before people arrive tonight," he messages. "We'll be taking them through the office to see everything. You can make a couple extra bucks. What do you say?"

"Sure." I'm nervous, but if I'm in the back, things will be fine.

"Let Annie know I've taken you so she doesn't sit around and wait."

"I'll tell her," I say.

When we drive to the office, Dad talks about the people coming in from out of state. And how this deal is going to grow the business. And thank you, Sarah, thank you for helping me.

"Listen," he says. "When this is done, we're doing something as a family. Just the four of us. A vacation. No phones. Just our family."

Tears form in Dad's eyes.

"I owe you an apology too, Sarah."

Then he pulls me close in a hug.

I don't speak. Just feel the warmth of his arms.

"Will you be okay?" he asks, releasing me.

"Sure," I say.

"I'll come back to pick you up later," he says.

I nod and take the box of paperwork from his car and into the building.

Paul is behind glass walls with a young couple who have a baby in a car seat. Has he sold them a house already? They all look pretty thrilled.

I can smell coffee and someone, somewhere, has made popcorn.

I'm working away not thinking of anything really, except the violin piece that I can't get out of my head. My fingering, bow strokes, timing all play over and over in my brain. I have to admit, it sounds pretty good. Both in real life and in my mind.

I've been working at least an hour when Emma Jean stops in the room.

"Hey, Sarah," she says. "Have you seen your father?" She languishes against the doorjamb, her long blonde hair (extensions, I'm sure) falling forward and says, "I've been searching for him all day."

Just like that, with the way she asks, I wonder if more is going on with Emma Jean and Dad than selling houses. I think of the times I've seen them together here in the office: Her smiling when he comes in the room. Her hand on his arm when they're together. All the times he's left the house late at night. All the phone calls. All the messages.

Were they to Emma Jean?

A family vacation.

Family time.

My fingers tremble, and the paper in my hands shakes.

Is she having an affair with my father? I think of that card. His apology last night. The promises now. Could this be?

Does Mom know?

Would Dad do that?

And what about Annie?

Does Annie know something I don't?

"Sarah?"

"I don't know," I say. "I mean. The airport." I can't look at her without thinking … without thinking icky things.

"That's right. The possible merger."

How could she forget that? It's all Dad's been talking about. I bet the rest of the office has been talking as well. It means big things for everyone. Expansion. More money.

"Gotta go," I say. I push past Emma Jean.

There's really no place to go with my handful of papers, so I hurry to the bathroom. My father with this woman? It bothers me so much that I hurry into a stall and do all I can to calm my stomach. Then I pull on my coat and leave the building. I realize those papers are still on the counter in the restroom. Not good. Though I was nearly done filing.

I'm going to get fired, but I don't care.

I gotta go.

I walk down Main, climbing over snowbanks as the wind tears at me, wishing the sidewalks were clearer. Wishing I didn't know what I think I know. Wondering how Mom will feel. Something has grabbed my guts, and maybe our lives will never be the same again, hugs and promises and whatever. And just when I thought they were getting better.

The traffic is horrible. A car beeps as it zooms past. Already my cheeks are numb and my ears burn. I should have called Annie. Asked her to give me a ride home.

Everything, everything whirring through my mind points to an affair.

I try to calm the vomit feel in my stomach.

Is this why Annie hates working there?

I breathe deep the air that might freeze my lungs, the air that smells of exhaust.

A red BMW pulls up next to a snowbank and I walk like I can't see it. The window rolls down and there's David. He's smiling. Wasn't he in the office?

"Hey, Sarah," David says. "What are you doing out here? The weather's awful."

That's a good question. I have no idea why I've left. I just know I have to get home. I'm sick with worry. Or just plain sick.

"Are you headed to your place?"

I nod.

"And there's no one here to take you?"

I shrug.

A semi passes, splashing slush in my direction. There's a baby seat in the back of David's car.

"I can take you home if you want. I have to go pick up my kids from the sitter anyway — Lisa has to work late. Do you want me to take you?"

I don't answer. A moment later I hear the door unlock. I climb into the car. He turns the heat on high and we drive off.

annie

When I get home from school
the house is quiet.
The perfect kind of
quiet.
Mom is gone
(finalizing things? Picking up
last-minute items?) and Sarah
must still be at work.

I go into the kitchen and
do what I do best.
Make myself
salmon,
couscous,
I even steam carrots and Brussels sprouts.
I pile the food onto my plate, go into the living room,
light the fireplace,
and sit alone
to eat.

annie

"Where's Sarah?"
Mom wants to know.

I'm at the piano.
Going through what we'll play.
Thinking about the change
in Dad.
Letting the music carry me.
Playing.
I've missed the piano. It's
taking me awhile to
get used to the keys again.
They are cool, foreign,
under my fingers.
Can't believe it's been almost a year
since I played
not including this last-minute practice.
But it's like being on a bike.
I remember
and love
the feel of this.

230

"Huh?"

"Your sister?
She's not at the office.
Not with Dad at the airport."

My heart flutters.
Sarah's missing?
She wasn't home for dinner.
I close the piano then
call her phone, but she doesn't answer.
There's a just-like-that
headache behind my eyes.

I check her room
panic trying to control me
and see her in bed.

sarah

What are you doing in here?" Annie asks. From the tone of her voice I can't tell if she's mad or worried. "Why are you in bed?" She sits on the edge of my mattress.

I roll over. "It's Emma Jean and Dad, isn't it?"

"What?" Annie sounds confused.

"They're sleeping together, aren't they?"

It's not a question, because by now I'm sure. I pull the covers over my head. Feel four years old.

"Does Mom know?"

In the darkness I peer out at Annie. For a moment, she looks like a ghost.

"Is that why you hate men?" I'm still under the covers. I can smell dinner. Can hear my father talking to Mom. When did he get home? "You found out about them, didn't you?"

Annie throws back her head and laughs. Flicks on the light. Doubles over. Keeps laughing. Then when she's wiping tears from her eyes, she kisses my forehead. "You are so cute. Dad would never do that. Let's go practice."

Relief floods me, then a spark of anger.

"What do you mean? I thought ..."

Annie grabs my hand in hers. "Dad is absolutely devoted to Mom," she says. "He's just been too busy with work. Remember our apology last night? I heard him talking to Mom, later. Telling her, essentially, what he told us. And Emma Jean? She can have her choice of men, and does. Nope. It's not that."

"But," I say. My face burns. I feel stupid to have made such a mistake. But thankful. Really thankful.

"Look, Dad can be a real jerk, but he's an honest jerk, unlike a lot of people at his company."

When we're done running through our piece, Annie closes the piano and says, "What in the world made you think Dad was having an affair?"

There's laughter in her voice and I tap her with the violin bow.

My face goes cold then hot. "You hate the office. Hate the parties."

Annie's still on the piano bench. She fiddles with the Mozart book, running the pages through her fingers. Dad is gone now, off for drinks. Mom went with him.

"Gone to relax," he told us, "before the party tomorrow."

"Look, he's been selfish. But right now I think he's just worried about growing the business." Annie straightens the music then flips off the light.

"I'm trying to figure things out," I say. I loosen the bow and put my violin in its case. It's dark now. And I'm hungry. Starving. That ride home with David wore me out. My supposed discovery did too.

"Emma Jean has a boyfriend who's two decades younger than she is. She's not interested in Dad."

"Are you sure?" I look my sister right in the eyes.

"Yes."

"Then why do you hate Mr. Freeman? And Dad's office."

Annie looks at me. Her mouth becomes a slash in her face. She takes a breath and says, "Wanna go running?"

saturday

sarah

"Sarah."

In my dream, Annie's voice, soft like the moon's light, comes into my mind.

"They found him," I said.

"Sarah."

"He wore a dress and used superglue to put on the beads." Mozart plays in the background, sounding a lot like when Annie sings.

"Sarah. Wake up!"

"Annie?" I sit up. "You scared me. What time is it?"

"Scoot over," she says.

I peer at the clock on my bedside table. It's 1:44. "Why so early?" I move, heavy with being tired, to let Annie crawl in bed with me.

"I'm ready to talk."

"Ready to talk about what?" And then I know.

This isn't Tommy stuff. It's something else.

She gets under the covers. She's cold. Like she's been outside cold.

"I can't sleep thinking about tonight. When everyone comes over, I mean."

"Why? Are you nervous?" I tuck the pillow behind my back.

She shakes her head. She smells like an old penny. She has been outside. Her feet are freezing.

"I had a bad dream," she says into my hair. She leans against the headboard too. Rests on my shoulder. She's shivering. "It was about him."

"Tommy Jones?"

"The man."

"Mr. Freeman?" My heart has stopped working. I should pound my chest. Make my heart beat again.

"No. He was just the first person I saw … after. I guess …" Annie's quiet. Then, "I wanted to be mad at someone. He was my best option. My first option. After."

"After what?" My mouth is dry. "Tell me."

She's quiet. I'm so awake I can hear the house moving in the cold. "What do you mean, the man?" I say. "A man? Not our neighbor?"

She shakes her head. Nods. Says, "Yes. No. Another man. This is … it's like … it's my fault. Like I had something to do with it. Because I did, you know? Because of the way I looked. Because …" She takes a breath, chews the air. "Because I said I liked him. Loved him."

"Okay." I wait, finish breathing. My heart slams in my head now, giving me an instant headache.

"I want you to know this. It's not Dad's fault."

"Dad?"

"He was always encouraging."

"Annie!"

"Listen, Sarah. This is hard to talk about."

I close my mouth. Keep it tight.

"At work. Daddy had me stay extra hours sometimes. And

238

sometimes." Annie stops talking. Takes my hand. "And David Carter was there."

"Okay."

"I had a crush on him and he said his wife didn't love him and he kissed me and I let him. More than once. And then, then in the office after everyone was gone, he wouldn't stop. And I was okay with it."

Annie's voice has gone low. Soft. Pained.

Maybe I'm dreaming. Maybe this isn't real. He took me home yesterday. He has that car seat. A wife. Children.

"I thought I loved him. Tommy had already tried stuff at school. There were the notes. And I was sure, sure David cared. He said he did. I think he still does. He still says he'll leave his wife." Annie sucks in air. "And he was a real man. You know? Not a kid."

A part of me wants to tell Annie to shut up. To not tell me this.

"He kissed me and touched me and said Lisa didn't love him and he knew that I did and I could show him and he would be gentle."

I'm numb. There's a bad taste in my mouth. Strong. Wicked.

"Do you believe me?"

I can hardly say the word. "Yes."

"When I saw how far it was going to go, I told him no. But he touched me anyway. He pushed up on me and breathed down my neck. We were in Dad's office on that sofa. The leather one. Then David's hands went everywhere. Everywhere, Sarah. And then ..."

I squeeze my eyes shut.

"He said he loved me. Said he wanted to be with me. And we did it. Had sex and I told him no, but he said it would be okay."

"Annie." My voice was all air. "Oh, Annie."

There's a pause that weighs as much as a boulder.

"Can you believe I lied?"

"How? How did you lie?" My words aren't whole. I crawl out of bed, try to take a few more breaths.

"By not staying a virgin. I was going to wait until marriage." She's crying then.

I think of Annie loud and proud about waiting. How can words hurt my brain? This does. It hurts my brain and my heart and my stomach.

"It happened a few times. I'd call him at home and he wouldn't answer. And then when he saw me at work ... he'd stay after hours and so would I."

"You were fifteen."

"Sarah? Are you okay?"

"No," I say. I go to the window and open it. "No, you were fifteen."

"And older."

I hesitate. "Is it over?"

"Not really. He still asks me to see him. Tells me he's doing me a favor being with me even though I'm fat."

"Are you kidding?"

"No."

We're both whispering.

"When was the last time you were with him?"

Annie rolls onto her back. "The end of last month. I decided I would never see him again. But he's still texting me."

Outside, the night is still. The sky is clear with icy stars dotting the darkness. Like a blanket, the cold pushes in through the screen. Fresh air settles my stomach but does nothing for the rising panic.

"Only you know," Annie says. "I'm talking with a school counselor. Though I haven't told her this. Not what happened. I haven't told anyone but you, Sarah. I'm not ready yet."

I put my hands on the windowsill. Press my forehead on the screen. I breathe deep to keep the nauseated feeling away. The screen smells musty. David Carter. With the little babies and the chatting. The BMW and the wife. The ride home and the small talk.

I go back to bed and crawl in beside Annie. "You have to tell," I say. "You said no. That's rape."

"I can't. I said yes later." Her voice is desperate. Frightened.

"You have to tell someone."

Cold air blows into the room. Papers rustle on my desk. Annie cries next to me. There's only the sound of her sobs. For several minutes she weeps, and I cry with her.

"I'm ashamed," Annie says after a while. "Like it was something I did. Like I took advantage of how I looked. Like I made it too easy. I let him care for me and I let me care for him."

"That's ridiculous," I say. "Look. Look. I'll tell Mom and Dad for you, okay?"

Annie's quiet. "I'm tired. You know what I mean?"

"Yeah," I say.

Annie says, "After the party, okay? I'll do it after the party. I don't want to ruin things for Dad."

"He'll be here," I say. "With Lisa."

"What's one more day?" Annie says. "We let Dad have his moment."

I don't answer.

"Okay?"

I nod. "You tell in twenty-four hours," I say, "or I do."

annie

The house is full
and I wait
wanting to see him
and hating him at the same time.

sarah

I stayed in my room all day. I had to. I can't eat. Can't think. Can't do anything. Annie's revelation makes me want to call the police. But I've promised. Not until this is over.

"Come on down with me," Annie says about seven thirty. "We need to mingle. Do the piece. Then you want to go for a drive?"

"Sure."

She's wearing black, like Mom requested. My sister looks … beautiful. She smiles at me, and I see she's scared.

"I'm sorry, Annie. I'm sorry." I clutch her close. We stand in my bedroom, together. Hugging. Maybe like when we were in the womb. "I'm sorry." I'm sick with anger at myself. I should have known. Twins know things. I should have stopped this. Stayed at the office with her. Not been so afraid.

"You have nothing to apologize for."

We go downstairs holding hands.

There are so many people that my anxiety rears its ugly head (cliché, but exactly what I'm feeling) and I can't swallow.

"It's okay," Annie says. She doesn't turn loose of my hand. Holds on. Guides me to the dining room where two caterers keep the table filled with food.

"Where're Mom and Dad?" she asks.

But I'm looking for David Carter.

And then I see him. He's watching us. Drinking a glass of wine. Watching Annie. His arm is around his pregnant wife.

I can't eat. Annie nibbles at a baby quiche. She socializes. Takes comments about her hair. Her piercings. Is she thinking of a tattoo? What are her goals?

I don't speak to anyone. Just sort of smile. I can't think. Move like a robot, jerky. David watches us where we go. Wherever we stop. Has he always done this? Or does he want my sister now?

Then Dad calls us in.

"My gorgeous daughters," he says. Dad grins. Mom hangs from his arm. I want to laugh that I thought he would have an affair.

But the real truth, it's worse.

Far worse.

"The halftime entertainment."

"Oh," I hear Emma Jean say. She's with a good-looking man in jeans and a sports coat. She's dressed in a gown. "These two girls are talented. Love this part of the evening. Everything else is so pretentious." I can see the diamond at her throat glitter. She nods at me. Smiles.

Somehow I'm standing at the piano. I test the strings on my violin. My knees shake.

Annie says, "We're almost done here, Sarah. Then we go."

I nod.

I hate this. Hate it!

She plays the first few chords.

I join her.

Close my eyes.

Think of the music.

The sound.

Rhythms.

Get lost in the arrangement, the perfection of the notes together. The way I feel as I play and, no, I won't think of anything. Not anything.

It's a longer piece. No one moves. Maybe they don't breathe the whole time. Maybe I don't either.

Then. It's over. Everyone claps. Dad hugs us, me first. I put away the violin. My hands shake hard now, like they waited until everything was over to come undone. Dad raises his champagne glass. Mom clinks her glass against his. Annie has moved to the edge of the living room.

Then David Carter is there.

Like a spirit.

I see him walk toward my sister, get too close.

His wife is talking to someone across the room from him.

I watch him lean over Annie. See her shake her head.

She looks at me.

"Leave her alone," I say. My voice is low. Flat. Crushed toward the carpet. This playing, this performance has taken everything out of me. I want to leave the house. Now.

David says something to Annie, who looks away, her face stricken.

"Leave her alone."

I don't even close the violin case, but step toward Annie, push past a guest from out of state. Dad won't like that, but I have to get to Annie.

"Leave her alone," I say again.

"Oh, Sarah," David says. And then. "A moment alone with your sister, please."

"Don't speak to her. Don't."

"It's okay, Sarah," Annie says. "I want to." Her eyes are huge. She bites at her bottom lip. Her face has lost all color.

"No!" My voice comes out far louder than I mean it. "I know," I say, "Daddy. Daddy!"

"Shhh, Sarah," David says. He's in my face. There are too many people here. Too much breathing. Sweating. Talking. Eating.

"Forget it, Annie. Never mind." David turns. Walks across the room.

"Sarah?" Annie says, and she's shaking her head in slow motion. Whispering *later. Later.*

"Dad!" I say.

sunday

sarah

I'm not sure how, but the news goes through the neighborhood like wildfire.

Someone drops off a basket of chocolates. Someone else a loaf of homemade bread. When I step out to get the paper, I find three cards in the mailbox. They're all addressed to Annie, all hand delivered.

Is it because the police showed up at the door? Because Dad nearly knocked out David's teeth? Because David's wife went screaming outside and drove off in that BMW?

All night I dreamed awful things. Annie kept crying out and I couldn't reach her.

Each time I woke up, I saw in my mind her chopped-off hair. Her black room. All that extra weight. I cried myself to sleep, twice.

This is how I want to be were like printed words in my head.

Mom and Dad and Annie left early with the plan to be gone for the day. "To see a lawyer," Dad said. "Then to the police station."

"Lock up," Mom said, and Annie grabbed me in a hug, her face splotchy from all the crying, her eyes swollen.

"Thank you," she said. Her breath was warm on my face and I wanted to cry again. "When I saw him, I just wanted to be with him. You saved me."

"We'll text you," Dad said.

All the air in the house leaves when my family drives away.

I walk from the kitchen to the hall, up to my room, to the basement and the pool table and back to the kitchen. I'm watching Judge Judy on YouTube when the doorbell chimes. I jump. Who can it be? A part of me wants to hide but it's noon, not midnight like it feels it should be, and this could be the police.

Instead Garret stands at the door. "I heard," he says.

A breeze rushes in the house, making me think there could be an end to winter in a month or two.

"Okay," I say.

"Can I come in?"

I hesitate.

"Sarah?"

"Oh, sure," I say and open the door wider. We stand in the foyer. Garret's hesitant, then he walks into the living room. There're still glasses all over the place and plates and even a platter of appetizers. Thai shrimp, my favorite. We didn't even get to the filet mignon with creamy mashed potatoes and asparagus.

Garret sits at the edge of an ottoman and I sit across from him. He's so cute I can hardly stand it.

"I wanna kill the guy," he says after a long minute where he's looking at his hands and I'm looking at him.

"I know." My voice is low.

"What's your family going to do?" He looks at me and I remember how I would kiss him for hours and how soft his lips are, and I miss those kisses so much.

"Dad's pressing charges," I say. A given, I know. "And David's been fired."

"Good." Then he says, "You know, Sarah, Annie is gonna get through this. I know she will. She's a lot like you. Tough."

"Like me?" I'm surprised. "Oh no. She's way better than me."

Garret touches my shoulder. Has a spark jumped from the fireplace to where his fingertips are?

"The two of you are a lot alike. Maybe not so much in looks, but in the way you both act. It's kinda cool. Twins who don't look exactly the same, but have personalities that are similar."

"That's not true," I say, though I'm warmed with the thought.

"Sure it is." Garret's hand is still on my shoulder. "Not in public. But when I've been with you, when it's just us, I see that confidence that Annie has."

"Really?" I open then close my mouth, and feel a smile playing at my lips. I want that. I want to be like my sister. "That's a real compliment," I say.

Can it be true?

"She won't be doing it so alone this time. None of us are planning on letting her. They're talking to a lawyer and all, and there are some things she has to work out by herself. But, you know, Mom and Dad and me? We're there for her now."

As I say these words (that feel empty), guilt clenches at my heart. Maybe if I hadn't spent so much time thinking Annie was fat and more time wondering why she was eating so much, things would be different. Maybe if I had listened sooner. Not left her alone.

Stayed at the office.

Looked outside of myself.

Thought of her.

Not been so afraid.

I take in a deep breath.

Garret grabs my hand, and the spark moves to my palm where he touches me. "Sarah."

I try to pull free, but he won't let me. Okay, I don't try that hard.

"Sarah."

"What?"

"I'm sorry. About everything. About what's happened with Annie. That I listened to my mom." He swallows. "That we haven't been together."

I don't say anything.

"I've missed you." Garret comes close. I can smell his after-shave. All I have to do is bury my head in his neck but instead I let him kiss me, his lips meeting mostly teeth because I'm smiling.

Then we're really kissing. Full on. And I missed him so much that my eyes fill with tears. His arms go around me. I hear his phone ring but he doesn't answer and we keep kissing. Keep kissing, standing now, so close and it's like we've never been apart.

The phone rings again.

"Your mom?" I ask, pulling away from him.

His face is flushed. He looks at his phone. His cheeks go redder. He nods.

I swallow. "Go home," I say, because I know right then this will never work. No matter how I want it to. Not this way. It can't.

And if Annie is going to be strong, so will I. I don't want to be, but I will.

"Sarah," he says.

"Go on."

He gives me one heartbreaking look. "Don't give up completely," he says.

His shoulders slump and he nods when I don't answer.

Then he's walking to the door and when he's off the porch, one hand in his pocket, the other holding the phone to his ear, I shut the door and cry.

For me.

For Garret.

But mostly, mostly for Annie.

sarah

When the rest of my family gets home, I wait for my sister to get out of the car.

"It's over," she says when she comes inside. She's weeping. So many tears today for our family. Too many.

Dad's furious. But he doesn't say much of anything except he's throwing the book at David Carter.

And that he's sorry. So sorry.

Mom says, "I should have known."

I think, *Me too.*

Annie falls into my arms.

"It was awful. The worst thing ever. The worst." She stops. Sobs. "Thank you," she says. "Oh, Sarah. Thank you."

I think over this last year. The hard stuff. The crap.

I know my sister. Annie can do anything.

sarah

And maybe I can too. Maybe, I can.